SELECTED SPEECHES
―――――――――――――――――― VOLUME 3

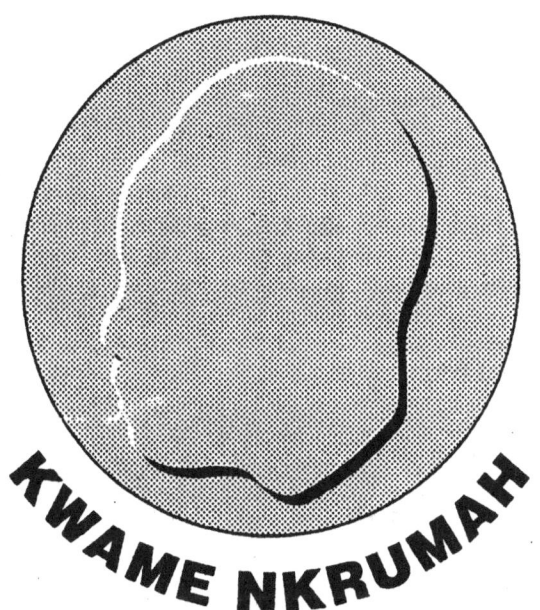

KWAME NKRUMAH

Compiled by Samuel Obeng

AFRAM PUBLICATIONS (GHANA) LTD.

Published by:

Afram Publications (Ghana) Ltd.,
P. O. Box M. 18,
Accra, Ghana,

© **The Republic of Ghana, 1960**

All Rights Reserved. No part of this book may be reprinted, or reproduced or utilized in any form or by any electronic, invented or other means, now known, including photocopying or recording, or any information storage and retrieval system, without permission in writing from Afram Publications (Ghana) Limited.

First Published 1997

ISBN 9964 70 203 5

Typeset by Damana Graphics

Printed by

FOREWORD

In the very first Volume of these Works published in 1973 it was suggested that, that Dr. Kwame Nkrumah, "a man who was (in his lifetime) so maligned, condemned and rejected by his own people should at his death be praised and loved so much and be finally accepted by his own people again, appears to testify to Nkrumah's charisma." This proposition has since it was made assumed greater significance in the light of later developments.

Since Dr. Kwame Nkrumah's death the Nkrumah factor has been very forcefully projected in politics and even in the daily lives of the people of Ghana and Africa. Nkrumah's influence has dominated the conduct of the majority of political parties in Ghana. These parties have all laid claim to descent from Dr. Kwame Nkrumah's Convention People's Party and to the Nkrumahist ideology.

Over the period Dr. Nkrumah's statute which was "brutalised" and shoved into obscurity has been re-created and displayed at the Mausoleum built for him in Accra. Furthermore his mortal remains have been transferred from his lowly Nkroful hometown and re-interred at this Mausoleum built and named after him at the very grounds in Accra where he proclaimed independence status for the then Gold Coast forty years ago.

Dr. Nkrumah was concerned with the unity and development of the whole of Ghana. He was concerned with the total welfare of its citizens; his was a vision of a welfare society where all in Ghana would enjoy a reasonably improved standard of life, hence his emphasis on the provision of social amenities like, health, and education. By this strategy he hoped to achieve accelerated economic development.

Nkrumah was passionately committed to the total liberation of the African continent and its eventual unity.

These concerns for domestic and international harmony and development are reflected in all his speeches, short and long, delivered at home and at numerous international fora. Some of the issues he addressed have over the years been resolved; but others like stability in Africa, improved social facilities for Ghana are still relevant.

When one talks of the indestructibility of the tongue it is in reference to the spoken word. In Dr. Kwame Nkrumah's speeches one finds this clearly illustrated. Hardly a national celebration passes without a reminder of Kwame's famous old Polo Grounds Speech declaring Ghana's Independence.

These volume of "Selected Speeches of Dr. Kwame Nkrumah" comes in the fortieth year of Ghana's Independence. It is hoped that the work will urge Ghanaians and friends of Ghana to push ahead with the principles and ideals which some fifty years and more ago inspired the struggle to build Ghana into a "middle level economy."

Accra
August, 1997

William Yaw Eduful
(Publicity Director)
Publicity Secretariate,
Flagstaff House, Accra.

PREFACE

Osagyefo Dr. Kwame Nkrumah had always been in the vanguard of what he himself called "The African Revolution." He had not only been at the centre of its political action, but had also articulated its ideology.

After Dr. Nkrumah's Government was overthrown by a military coup d' etat, on February 24, 1966, he was so much maligned, condemned and rejected by his own people that his books, speeches and pictures that could be reached were publicly burnt.

One afternoon in August, 1971 when I heard a news broadcast on Ghana Broadcasting Corporation Radio that an Act 380 of 28th August, 1971, had banned the use of any slogan by word or shiboleth, photograph, or policy document intended to revive the Convention People's Party (CPP) or its leader or chairman Dr. Kwame Nkrumah, I decided to gather the speeches from those who had them.

I wrote to the Government of the National Redemption Council when the obnoxious Act 380 of August, 1971 was repealed by NRCD 21 of 9th February, 1972, and was given a written permission to compile and publish the Speeches of Kwame Nkrumah.

Kwame Nkrumah's speeches, most of which are being presented together to the world in these volumes, still glow with the force of his personality, his conviction in the face of powerful opposition, his originality, his vision as well as his impatience when his expectations seemed delaying.

Nkrumah did not live to see all his dreams realised, but in his speeches and writings, he has left for posterity ideas which should inspire Africans and Black people everywhere.

It is my hope that readers of these volumes and future generations will derive from these pages the inspiration to fight to uproot the remnants of colonialism from the society.

Samuel Obeng
Compiler

Kumasi,
August, 1997

Dedicated to
politicians and Ex-servicemen
and Brothers and Sisters in the Diaspora
who laid down their lives
to make Ghana's Independence possible

"Truth forever on the scaffold,
Wrong forever on the throne
Yet that scaffold sways the future,
And, behind the dim unknown,
Standeth God within the shadow,
Keeping watch above his own."

—James Russel Lowell

CONTENTS

1. Law in Africa..1
2. Guide to Party Action..10
3. Gateway to Ghana...25
4. Opening of the Canadian Trade Fair.............................30
5. Africa Needs Her Farmers...33
6. Ghana Welcomes Foreign Enterprise............................37
7. The Laying of the Foundation Stone of City Hotel........43
8. The Ninth Annual National Delegate's Conference......48
9. Opening of the First Biennal Conference of the Ghana T.U.C...53
10. The Opening of Electricity and Water Supplies for Sunyani.......60
11. Appeals to National Workers.......................................62
12. Work and Happiness..65
13. Regrets and Forgiveness..71
14. Steps to Freedom...73
15. Opening of Police Headquarters................................102
16. Opening of British Science Exhibition......................106
17. Opening of the Accra Assembly................................110
18. Second Anniversary of Republic...............................138
19. Osagyefo's Peace Award..142
20. The Eleventh Party Congress.....................................145
21. Africa's Glorious Past..154
22. Some Notable Quotation..167

1

LAW IN AFRICA

CONFERENCE ON LEGAL EDUCATION AND FORMAL OPENING OF THE GHANA LAW SCHOOL

January 4, 1962

MR. CHAIRMAN, LADIES AND GENTLEMEN,

A friend of mine has always maintained that listening to lawyers is baffling, since you do not understand the terms they employ. But speaking to them is still more baffling, since you do not know the legal interpretation they place on your lay words! I myself was once almost initiated into this exclusive learned club. The fact that my initiation was not completed has at least saved you from a much longer and complicated address today. But, even though I consider myself a lay man, I think I can say a few words to you.

Speaking to this distinguished audience of lawyers, including many eminent ones, I hope that you will endeavour to strip your minds of too much law and interpret my words in their lay meanings! If you do so, I am sure no fireworks will be started in this hall by any attempt on your part to define the conduct of a lay man like me trying to speak on law to lawyers, as to whether such conduct amounted to larceny or fraud by false pretences!

Fortunately, I have a simple joint duty of opening these magnificent buildings of the Ghana School of Law and of declaring open the Conference on Legal Education in Africa–and this, happily, does not involve any dissertations on law!

What is pertinent to say here, however, is the fact in opening these buildings we are reviving part of our African culture and heritage interrupted by the colonial period, and we are not embarking on any new venture. Long before the foundation of the universities of the European continent, from which the modern civil codes of Europe have been evolved and long before the establishment of the universities and Inns of Court in the United Kingdom where the common law was taught and developed, law schools existed on African soil.

The Maliki School of Legal Thought, which had started as one of the more conservative trends, assumed a radical form. The universities south of Sahara, like the great University of Sankore at Timbuktu, were centres of university life and learning. In the fourteenth century a teacher of law who came to Timbuktu to teach law, returned to the University of Fez in Morocco saying that the city of Timbuktu was full of black lawyers and jurisconsults who knew more law than he did.

These centres of learning were of importance not only because they were among the foremost centres of culture of day, but also because they taught a system of law more advanced at that time than that existing in feudal Europe. In particular, they established the principle of the linking of law to social progress. The conception that law was a part of religion and therefore must serve all men equally, was an essential part of their contribution. African thinkers developed this idea into something larger and wider. Ibn Khaldun, a great African scholar who was also a distinguished lawyer and a Malikite chief justice in Cairo, had, as early as the fourteenth century, pointed out the importance of law being based upon what he called "social solidarity," but what we, in our day, would call "on the support of the masses". This theory of his is as true in our day as it was in his. Law, to e effective, must represent the will of the people and be so designed and administered as to forward the social purpose of the state. In Ghana we believe that it is only by socialist planning that we can industrialise and transform our country. Our lawyers therefore, if they are to understand the basic principles upon which the state is directed and why certain laws are enacted, repealed or amended by Parliament. The teaching of law is totally incomplete if it is not accompanied by a background of economic, social and political science, and even politics, science and technology.

The teaching of law in Africa would also be totally incomplete if it did not include a study of African law. The understanding of the basic principles of customary law is particularly important in that it is necessary to grasp the process by which this law has responded to economic and social changes, and the valuable contribution which it can make to legal thinking.

Well over fifty years ago, one of the greatest of our lawyers, John Mensah Sarbah, contributed a preface to a book on Colonial Gold Coast Law published at the expense of Sarbah and his Ghanaian friends, and written by a British colonial judge of the day, Hayes Redwar. Sarbah began his preface with these words:–

> *The African social system is communistic and has been built up gradually, and as a race should grow its own laws just as an animal must grow its own skeleton, so as to meet its own special requirements, so has native customary law grow.*
>
> *The conflict between African communism and European individualism confronts the legislative reformer in the British West African Colonies, who, when he essays to destroy, should either provide an adequate substitute, or give the people affected by his new enactment facilities to invent their own restraints suitable to their changed condition. It is doubtful whether the official mind has yet grasped thoroughly the fact that the underlying principle of the aboriginal social system is the sense of duty to performed, respect to be paid to the aged, and obedience to the man in authority, whether head of family, headman of a town or chief of a tribe. To encourage the individual to compete with his neighbour in the performance of work, and to continue to take interest in the progress of his community is wise; but to insist on individualism to the extent of encouraging selfishness, and destroying what is undoubtedly good and beneficial in the native's institutions, is hardly commendable.*
>
> *In the African social system the formation of a pauper class in unknown, nor is there antagonism of class against class. Indeed, recognition by promotion to office and public position in the community is to many a sufficient incentive to effort and perseverance.*
>
> *Dealing with individualism, one should not fail to develop in all the various sides of the native's character, in other words, aim at levelling up; divert to proper use the energy and enthusiasm shown in company fights; and definitely get rid of the idea that aboriginal administration is hopelessly saturated with cruelty and inextricably*

permeated with corruption, and therefore should be destroyed. And, in this connection, one should recollect that the ancient Briton at a certain period seemed to the Romans no less unpromising. In fact Cicero, writing to his friend Atticus, recommends him not so procure his slaves from Britain, 'because they are so stupid and utterly incapable of being taught, that they are unfit to form a part of the household of Atticus.'

All that Mensah Sarbah is trying to say is that our law must embody our traditional social attitudes of communal endeavour, of a classless society and of mutual self help so as to avoid the narrow interpretation of man's duties to the community and the a state, found so often in Western law.

For example, the emphasis laid by nineteenth century judges in Britain and in the United States on the rights of property, are entirely inappropriate in Ghanaian conditions.

There is a ringing challenge to African lawyers today. African law in Africa was declared foreign law for the convenience of colonial administration, which found the administration of justice cumbersome by reason of the vast variations in local and tribal custom. African law had to be proved in court by experts. But no law can be foreign to its own land and country, and African lawyers, particularly in the independent African states, must quickly find a way to reverse this juridical travesty.

The law must fight its way forward in the general reconstruction of African action and thought and help to remould the generally distorted African picture in all other fields of life. This is not an easy task, for African lawyers will have to do effective research into the basic concepts of African law, clothe such concepts with living reality and give the African a legal standard upon which African legal history in its various compartments could be hopefully built up.

Law does not operate in a vacuum. Its importance must be related to the overall importance of the people, that is to say, the state.

Law, like all other subjects and perhaps more than most, must be practically applied. I am convinced that its application, like that of other subjects, must be relative. No absolute application of the knowledge of law could therefore be of use either to the lawyer himself or to his client or clients.

Two Ghanaian lawyers trained in the United Kingdom were once arguing on property in my presence. It was Ghanaian property. One of them, newly arrived, referred to something called Free Tail. At once the other exclaimed: "Free Tail? Here in Ghana? You must be dreaming!" The Free Tail lawyer knew of Free Tail in English Law and believed, therefore, that there must be a Free Tail in Ghanaian Law. But our lawyers must do their utmost to serve Africa in the context of our own conditions and circumstances, our traditions and culture, our hopes and aspirations.

It is important that we realise the great advantages which may result from a progressive and organised development of common law legal institutions. In this matter I took the initiative early this year of proposing to the United Kingdom Government that there should be some much more organised method for the giving of legal technical aid and for the making known of the law reform taking place in various parts of the Commonwealth.

In making these proposals I had in mind the great quantity of legal reform and investigation which we have carried out in Ghana since independence. These have all been based upon a close study of Ghanaian conditions and are therefore likely to contain ideas and principals suitable for other emergent common law countries. I hope that all our visitors from abroad will take away with them copies of our reports on the reform of Company Law and on the establishment of a new law of insolvency, which are examples of the constructive legal thinking which is being done in Ghana to-day and which also illustrate how we have been able to utilise the experience of foreign exports to assist in involving highly technical and difficult legal problems.

I have recently received a letter from Mr. Macmillan welcoming the ideas, offering assistance and making a number of positive and concrete suggestions on which the United Kingdom Government are consulting other Commonwealth Governments. I should therefore like to take this occasion to put on record our sincere thanks to the United Kingdom Prime Minister and Government for their interest and assistance in this proposal, which seems to me an admirable example of the way in which Commonwealth countries can co-operate. I hope, however, that the scheme, when finalised, will be of a kind in which all countries whose legal systems derive in whole or in part from the common law may participate.

In reforming our own laws and we have sought technical assistance from Commonwealth countries, the Irish Republic and the United States of America. In our new legislation, we have adopted a number of local principals advocated by such bodies as the New York State Law Revision Committee. Such outside help is of value provided, of course, that the basic principle–that all our laws must be designed to meet the needs and aspirations of our people–is never forgotten.

Indeed, the object of our founding a law school and establishing a law faculty at the University, was to teach law appropriate to Ghana and not the law and the political thinking of any other country, however appropriated that law and political thinking might be in that particular country. Naturally, since we have inherited the common lay system from the United Kingdom and since much of our written law is founded upon Acts of the United Kingdom Parliament and upon ordinances of the colonial days, much of the legal instruction given us was based upon English and Commonwealth law.

It is therefore natural that we should look in the main for law teachers who will have been trained in English Law as the duty of these teachers not to represent English Law as the standard to which we must necessarily conform or as containing fixed and rigid principles from which we must never depart. They must regard it rather as a foundation from which to build in a form adapted to our own social system. We must broaden the scope of law taught. In a developing country, the first priority is not for lawyers trained to conduct litigation between wealthy individuals.

Unfortunately, colonial conditions produced just this type of lawyer, and our own colonial legal system resulted in, for example, "land" cases between chiefs involving law suit after law suit.

In the old days, one case alone might go on appeal to the Privy

Council two or even three times upon one or other aspect of the matter and perhaps take up to twelve years before a final decision was reached. In consequence, there was no certainty as to the legal position and the revenues of the traditional authorities involved were wasted in the working of a fantastically cumbersome, expensive and dilatory process. Land disputes of this nature should be settled, as our law now permits, by appropriate actions by the administration. The land litigation of the past should serve as a warning of the disastrous consequences of attempting to apply English legal forms to issues for which they were never intended.

The lawyers needed in a developing state are, in the first place, those trained to assist the ordinary man and woman in his every day legal problems and particularly in the new problems likely to arise through industrialisation. For example, lawyers are required by the trade union movement to assist in making effective agreements with employers and seeing to it that the individual trade unionist obtains what is legally due to him if he is injured at work or is illegally dismissed. In the same way, lawyers are required throughout the country so that in same towns and villages, inexpensive but good advice can be had by the ordinary man and woman so that they are not put at a disadvantage in dealing with a wealthy trading or commercial firm.

This is a very different conception to that of the lawyer of colonial days who lived in the big towns and spent most of his time in court or chambers dealing with a very restricted class of client. In consequence of the nature if his work, he was very liable to become subconsciously an exponent of the views of colonial economic interests.

Secondly, and perhaps most important of all, we need lawyers in the service of the state, to deal with treaties and commercial agreements and with questions of private and public international law.

A modern state requires also in its public services an increasing number of persons with a legal education, not only as advisers and legal technicians, but also in the day to day administration of the country.

You all know my general views, and it is therefore not necessary for me to elaborate what I have always stressed on innumerable occasions, namely, the need for African unity. This, however, is not only a political question. It is also a matter of constantly increasing inter-African economic and cultural relations. Thus, Ghanaian lawyers must became well acquainted with the law of other African countries and must be taught at least the principles of civil and administrative law as obtaining in may African states through their adoption of a system based on the great European continental codes of the nineteenth century.

In my view, legal education in Africa should be founded on a grasp of the systems of law which exist in our continent to-day. It must also be based upon a sound knowledge of progressive economic and social theory. We must avoid the tendency to suppose that the form in which law is administered is more important than the content of the law. Law is converted into a reactionary force once it is regarded as an abstract conception, which is in some mysterious way universally applicable without regard to the being to the economic and social conditions of the country in which it is being applied. The reserve is true. The law should be the legal expression of the political, economic and social and conditions of the people and of their aims for progress. It is the height of absurdity to attempt to assess the legal institutions of any country by adopting a formalistic yardstick which completely disregards the material content of the law and measures justice or injustice solely by procedural rules. Unfortunately such an approach too often marks the attitude of even the most eminent lawyers towards people with whose economic needs and social and political aims they do not see eye to eye.

This law school, whose buildings I am formally opening today, was founded less that two years after Ghana became independent, to prepare students to become lawyers. Our initiative in this is proof of our belief in legality and our realisation of the need for a dynamic approach to legal teaching.

The object of the school is to give both full and part time tuition in law so that those who had wished to become lawyers but who could not in the past afford the large sums required to study at the Inns of Court in London, can now qualify. It will thus result in future generations of Ghanaian lawyers obtaining their qualifications in their own country.

I am opening this school of law and throwing open its doors not to Ghanaian students alone, but also to African students everywhere who may wish to study law here.

In my second task–that of opening the conference–I should like to express my appreciation of the interest shown by so many eminent members of the legal profession of other countries who have done us the honour of coming to participate in this conference. I am certain that your deliberations will be directed towards achieving practical results and in particular to working out a common approach to the study of law so that we may better understand each others' legal institutions and practice. Above all, any narrow view of legal teaching should be excluded.

Africa needs many lawyers, always provided–and this is an essential proviso–that they are trained for the need of their peoples. They are needed not only on the bench and at the bar. They are needed in every sphere of government, whether national or local. They are needed equally in industry and commerce, and our plans for state industrial and agricultural development will require the services, among others, of lawyers. The subjects taught and the methods of teaching should therefore be positively directed towards training lawyers to serve their communities.

And now, Mr. Chairman, Ladies and Gentlemen, I have much pleasure in declaring these buildings of the Ghana School of Law, and the Conference on Legal Education in Africa, formally opened.

2

GUIDE TO PARTY ACTION

SEMINAR AT THE KWAME NKRUMAH INSTITUTE OF IDEOLOGICAL STUDIES

Winneba
February 3, 1962

COMRADES,

This is the first Party Seminar of its kind to be held here since this Institute was opened. For this reason, I thought I would open it myself and take an active part in its deliberations.

We have reached a stage in the life of our Party and the Nation when we cannot expect to move forward on mere sentiment and emotion. If we expect to move forward, we have to face fact and reality.

You have gathered here as members of the Central Committee, as members of our great Party, as Ministers of State, as Regional Commissioners, as Deputy Ministers, Party officials and District Commissioners. In short, the Party and the Government are fully represented here to-day. We represent the Party, we represent the Government, we represent the Nation and we represent the people. As such, this meeting is no ordinary meeting, and we must emerge from it fortified and determined to carry through the task and programme before us.

As I have already stated, our Party cannot afford to go forward from the stage it now finds itself, in ignorance. It must equip itself with the requisite knowledge that should make it capable not only of giving the political direction it must give to the people, but also to give the necessary expert guidance in our task of socialist reconstruction of our country. The main theme for our discussion here should centre around Party education, Party organisation and Party ideology, and the relation of these to the State and the Government.

Less than a fortnight ago, the Central Committee announced the delimitation of the Party Study Groups. No doubt this announcement must have caused some surprise since we have been talking about the intensification of Party educational work. The Central Committee's decision, Comrades, was taken after a most careful consideration and in best interest of Party education. If you would look back a little, you would surely find that the work of Party education was formerly undertaken by the NASSO. This was a body of socialist students in the Party devoted to the ideals of socialism and engaged in the study of Party affairs, including the Party Constitution. The NASSO was most useful, but when the time came and it was considered that its work was done, the Central Committee transformed it into Party Study Groups. You will note that these metamorphoses and transformations are not concerned with aims and principles, but with tactics. Let us not forget that Marxism is not a dogma but a guide to action.

Other things being equal, the Central Committee considers that the NASSO and the Party Study Groups have done their work and done it very well. They have stirred up great enthusiasm in the field of Party education and their activities have led to the general raising of the standard of enlightenment among the rank and file of the Party. Nevertheless, the time has come when Party education should be carried forward to its final stage—the stage of mass Party education. General Party education must reach the masses at the base.

We must now go to the masses and give them help to understand the affairs of our great Party and the Nation by providing them with the necessary knowledge for thought and action.

The Party has defined a social purpose and it is committed to socialism and to the ideology of Nkrumaism. And I take it to mean that when you talk of Nkrumaism, you mean the name or term given to the consistent ideological policies followed and taught by Kwame Nkrumah. These are contained in his speeches, in his theoretical writings and stated ideas and principles. You also mean that Nkrumaism, in order to be Nkruma-istic must be related to scientific socialism. To be successful, however, this ideology must

(a) be all-pervading, and while its theories in full can only be developed in and around the Party leadership, it influence in some form all education and indeed, all thinking and action;

(b) be not only a statement of aims and principles, but must also provide the intellectual tools by which these aims are achieved, and must concentrate on all constructive thinking around achieving those aims, and,

(c) offer the ordinary man and woman some concrete, tangible and realisable hope of better life within his or her lifetime.

With this ideology there should be full-scale intellectual, education and organisation attack on all aspects of colonialism, neo-colonialism and imperialism. These are not just mere words. They are concrete manifestations of a world outlook. Colonialism is that aspect of imperialism which in a territory with an alien government, that government controls the social, economic and political life of the people it governs. Neo-colonialism is the granting of political independence minus economic independence, that is to say, independence that makes a State politically free but dependent upon the colonial powers economically. Imperialism is nothing but finance capital run wild in countries other than its own.

Of these three, neo-colonialism is the most dangerous not only to the African Liberation Movement as a whole, but also to the independence and unity of Africa. Without going into its philosophy, here are some of its techniques:

(a) To produce a small educated African "elite" as prospective rulers, whether or not they have the support of the masses.
(b) To educate this "elite" so that they would automatically accept, as part of the natural order of things, the colonial relationship, and defend it in the name of "justice", "political liberty" and "democracy".
(c) To prevent by organisational and ideological means, any concentration of power, without which change is impossible.
(d) While paying lip service to democracy, to exclude by organisational and ideological methods, the representatives of the mass of the people for any real control over the State.
(e) To exclude, by all possible means, any teaching which might lead to the advancement and practice of revolutionary ideas.

These are the political techniques which neo-colonialism is employing in order to tighten its economic control of the territory through a puppet "elite".

The economics of neo-colonialism is obvious. It gives fake aid to the newly independent country which makes that country virtually dependent economically on the colonial power. Thus it becomes a client state of the colonial power, serving as the producer or raw material, the price of which is determined by the colonial power.

How do we proceed then? I would like to suggest this approach: the Secretariat of the Bureau of Party Education must now go to the people; it must go to the ward, town and village branches as well as to the special branch created in the offices, shop, factories, state farms, corporations and other places of employment, carrying its work to our general membership. It must go to the primary schools through the Young Pioneers; it must go to the secondary schools, colleges and universities. And here it is proper that we confine Party Study Groups to secondary schools, colleges and universities. In this connection, I suggest that Education Secretaries should be appointed wherever a Party branch is established, and these should undertake Party educational work in addition to their normal duties.

Branch Education Secretaries must be taken in hand in a most serious manner by the Bureau of Party Education, so as to ensure that they understand thoroughly the tenets and basic principles of the Party ideology.

A proper plan of work and timetable should be formulated for this work, and tuition and discussion should be carried on both in the local languages and in English.

Periodically a meeting of all Branch Secretaries and Branch Educational Secretaries should be held at Flagstaff House, or at such other place as may be decided, in order that they may be addressed by leading members in ideological education on appropriate subjects. This periodical meeting should take the place of the Party Study Groups meeting at Flagstaff House. In addition to the Branch Secretary and Branch Education Secretary, party wards, branches and special branches should be allowed to send to such meetings not more than five chosen Party members. This will give opportunity to all members of a branch to present, at our time or another, at these periodical educational meetings which can conveniently be called the Party Educational Conference.

The Party Educational Conference should be held at three levels: National—which will invariably take place in Accra; Regional—which will take place at Regional Headquarters; and District–which should be held at District Headquarters. These Party Educational Conferences should not be confused with the Party National, Regional and District Conference.

Similarly, there should be appointed Regional and District Educational Party Secretaries whose responsibilities will be the proper co-ordination and supervision of all Party education work in a given Region or District. It is my hope that these steps, when taken will go a long way towards facilitating the work of mass Party education.

Let me now turn to other matters. The future of Ghana depends upon the youth, and if the Party is to achieve any worthwhile results by making sure of the future national trend, then it must take positive steps to inculcate in the minds of the nation's youth the ideology of the Party. Only by this way can we envisage the continuity of our line of thought and action long after many of us are gone.

The youth must be imbued not only with a keen spirit of patriotism, but also with a sense of lofty socialist ideas which will enable them to think and in the best interests if the community as a whole and not in the interest of themselves as individuals.

Another subject of importance is the Party Rally, Hitherto, Party Rallies have been held without proper preparation. The Propaganda Unit does very useful work in drawing the crowds and organising them into a good audience, but this apart, no plan appears to be made in regard to speakers or their subjects. The result is that quite often persons have spoken on subjects on which neither the Party nor the Government have given any line, and which has resulted as a shock not only to the Party or Government authority, but also to the audience, Such a state of affairs must be corrected.

In future, all Party Rallies should be covered by proper agenda approved by the Regional or District Secretaries, whose-ever responsibility this may be. Party functionaries responsible for organising rallies will have to arrange for speakers to be properly briefed on the subjects of their address. Where it is not possible to get a local speaker on a particular subject, arrangements must be made with Party Headquarters to provide speakers in respect of that subject. Regional Commissioners and Regional Secretaries of the Party will bear a special responsibility for directing the activities of the Party in regard to rallies.

In any case, the old time "say anything" sort of attitude, which has long characterised the speeches of Comrades at Party Rallies, must have a new orientation. The masses nowadays have no applause for demagogues. They want to hear something useful and sensible; to help them along in their daily life. They want to be told the actual facts of a situation.

I now come to general Party organisation. We often talk of the integral parts of our great party, but not many of us find time to examine the real position as regards these various organisations comprising the Party. The integral organisation which primarily combine to form the Convention People's Party consist of:

(1) The Trades Union Congress;
(2) The United Ghana Farmers Council;
(3) The National Council of Ghana Women;
(4) The Ghana Young Pioneers; and
(5) The Co-operative Movement.

All these bodies have their various functions in the particular aspect of our national life in which they operate, but there is one strain running through all of them, which is basic and fundamental, namely, the membership of the Convention People's Party. Whatever they do, the charter of the Convention people's Party must be clearly manifested for all to see. They all have a single guiding light, the guiding light of our party ideology. This light must be kept bright and full of lustre and must on no account be allowed to dim, for, as soon as this happens, we are bound to find ourselves in difficulties.

Let all Comrades remember, whether we be Trade Unionists,

whether we be Farmers, whether we be members of the Women's Council or of the Young Pioneers, that the dominant character which should take precedence in all that we do is the character of the membership of the Convention People's Party. This character is the guiding force of our Ghanaian life and existence and constitutes the bulwark against national treachery, intrigue, subversion and other un-Ghanaian activities.

The next category of Party organisation includes the Workers' Brigade and the State Construction Workers, which also, directly but nonetheless effectively, bolster the Party structure. Why shouldn't the workers of the State, who are composed mainly of the labourer group, be put into uniform? This would give them an added incentive to serve the State, a reason to feel proud of their service and sense of belonging.

They can be employed on various national jobs by the State Construction Corporations. This will eliminate the present element of idleness which takes place when a particular job is completed and the workers await the assignment of another job.

The Asafu Companies also, the members of which are almost all members of the Party individually, will come within this category. They should be properly uniformed and perform their traditional role in a modern manner.

Another group of workers whom we are now call "Watchmen" will have a new orientation and come under this category. And why shouldn't they also be dressed in a smart uniform and be renamed "Civil Guards?"

All this will lead to one useful result—discipline. The whole nation from the President downwards will form on regiment of disciplined citizens. In this way, we shall move forward with great confidence, stepping ahead ever firmly with a keen sense of purpose and direction.

All these organisation must form a solid forward movement with a new outlook, which must keep constant vigilance to make it impossible for anyone, whether from inside or from without, to compromise the independence of our country.

I would now like to draw your attention to some matters to which I have had occasion to refer from time to time, namely: rumour-mongering, anonymous letter writing, deliberate manufacture of destructive stories about Comrades, invidious whispering campaigns, loose talk and character assassination. All these tend to obstruct the steady progress of our Party and the Nation.

Day in and day out, my desk is literally flooded with hundreds of letters–mostly synonymous–sent in a spiteful campaign aimed at discrediting this or that individual. Those who do this sort of thing, if they are Party members, are not worthy to hold Party cards. Party members should not indulge in this practice.

Sometimes the Police have been able to unearth some of these enemies of the Nation and have brought them to book, but by and large, this useless, demoralising and unprofitable activity continues, and I wish to appeal to all Comrades to keep their eyes and ears open wide so that we may effectively check this wicked practice. If a Party member—or any other citizen, for that matter—discovers some malpractice or other wrong deeds being committed, then he should report on this in the proper manner and bring the matter to the notice of the proper authority. If you believe that what you write is the truth, then you should have no fear to sign your name. All anonymous correspondence which comes my way goes immediately into the wastepaper basket, which is the only place for the work of such cowards, mischief-makers or crack-pots.

Again, take the practice of using other people's names for the purpose of collecting money. Some Comrades make it their habit to go around the country in a bid to get rich quick by threatening people and collecting money from them in the names of Party Comrades. This is a most vicious and shameful; practice and one that must be ruthlessly and severely punished when discovered. It is your responsibility to see that this is checked.

Another malpractice which undermines the efficiency of the Party work, is the manufacture of lying propaganda against men in key positions. This has the result of undermining the confidence of such persons in themselves and therefore of impairing their ability and efficiency, since they constantly live in fear. Conversely, some Party members in high positions use their position to threaten and intimidate those whom they are trying to influence.

These are very dangerous practices and make the Party and the Nation lose ground.

Personally, I do not see why Comrades in key positions should allow themselves to be effected by such talk; and equally, I do not understand why others should allow themselves to be threatened and intimidated by a lot of bragging and boasting. If a Comrade's hands are clean, then surely he must have nothing to fear, no matter how many stories of dismissal and demotion are invented about him, or how frightening may be the threats hurled at him. A Party member protects himself with his own integrity and honesty and by his efficiency. By doing so, and provided his hands are clean, he will maintain his confidence and carry on, knowing that his actions are above suspicion and that his character is unassailable.

It is not necessary for me to dwell at length on the importance of honesty and service. The abuse of power through dishonesty is an abomination. The misuse of office for selfish ends is a crime against the Party and the State, and therefore a greater abomination. The Convention People's Party is the servant of people, and therefore the men whom it puts into office and power must use opportunity to serve the people, remembering at all times that selfless and loyal service is a reward in itself.

I do not know of any greater satisfaction than honest and efficient service rendered to the people in the best interest of all people. I should think that is enough reward for the gratification of our inner self, but when we forget ourselves and think of office, wealth and power as personal instruments meant to be used for the glorification of self and for the attainment of our individual purposes, then we falter in our charge and fail the Party and the people.

I think the life of our community must be organised right at its base, that is to say, at the village level. It is true that Local Government has been organised at the village level, but only by grouping a number of villages to form an administrative unit. The internal life of particular villages, therefore, remains substantially unadministered, and I believe the time has now come for us to tackle this problem in a fortnight manner.

A solution can be found in the formation of village committees which will be granted governmental authority for the administration of the village. In this respect a village committee can be made of the Chairman of the village Party branch, the Secretary and five other appointed members. The Odikro of a particular village will become the President of the village committee in the same way as higher Chiefs occupy the office of President of City and other Councils for ceremonial purposes only.

The real responsibility for the administration of a village will remain with the other members of the committee who, as I have said, will comprise the Party representative of the village. The Party and the Government will then be able to rest content that State administration goes down right to the town and village levels and makes the ordinary worker, farmer and peasant a participant in the government of the country.

The value of all the organisational wings of he Party and the National Assembly is that they broaden the basis of support for the leadership. The Party naturally must be the main basis from which the leadership draws its strength, and it is therefore important that support is mobilised from as many quarters as possible. The need for central leadership must permeate all the activities of the State. This involves not only those conducted through the classical apparatus, that is, the civil service, the judiciary, the armed forces and the police, but also those conducted through the central banks, government boards and corporations and indeed, by the Party itself.

This seminar also gives me the opportunity to lay emphasis on the importance of human relations, and in this respect, I am addressing myself particularly to Minister, Deputy Ministers and all others in authority. It is vital that our relationship with those who serve under you is of the most harmonious kind. It is not enough to see that their official work is properly done. You must also take an interest in their personal lives, show sympathy for their difficulties and, where possible, offer help. The colonialist attitude of "lording it" over subordinate s pays no dividends at all. The way to get results is to keep a man in the picture, take an interest in the job he is doing, correct him if he is wrong, praise him if he excels himself, let him feel that he is a vital part of the machinery, so that his self-respect and dignity are upheld. If, however, this personal approach fails on account of an arrogant or unco-operative attitude of the person concerned, then exercise no mercy.

Ministers, Regional and District Commissioners and all others in responsible positions, should keep contact with their staff by visiting their offices as often as possible, having homely chats with them and making them appreciate the fact that no matter the difference in official status, a Ministers and a Messenger are both Ghanaians and both Human beings. I am not advocating negative familiarity: that only spells ruin. What I am advocating is the cultivation of a sincere interest in one another as fellow beings and, arising from that, a mutual interest in the welfare of the State.

Nothing can be more disastrous both to the individual and to the State than a man who becomes so discouraged in his work and so negative in his attitude to life, that he carries out his duties like an automaton—disinterested. He acts like an automaton because he is treated like one. So little interest is taken in a the work he turns out that he shrugs his shoulders and says: "Why should I bother? I get paid for it." After all, he is human.

Ministers and all those holding responsible positions, should hold regular discussion with their secretaries and those working with them, and acquaint them with the problems of their Ministers and with national problems so that they become interested in the affairs of State, proud to be taken into the confidence of their superiors and keen to prove their worth.

One subject which should occupy your attention during these discussions is the subject of the Ghanaian attitude to State property. Under the colonial regime, the people were made to feel so remote from the Government and so divorced from it, that they grew up with the idea that the Government and the people were two different entities. In those days, Government property was treated with deliberate negligence, scant attention or dishonesty. Unhappily, this attitude has, harm to a great extent, remained, and it is causing a good deal of harm to our society to-day.

It must be clearly understood by everyone that the people and the Government are one, and that property acquired by Government is State property, that is to say property belonging to the people and property for which the people are responsible. So if a person is put in charge of a particular property that belongs to the State, that is, to the people, he is guarding that property on behalf of himself and the people, who each have a stake in it. It is in his interest, therefore, to guard and preserve it with the greatest care and attention.

This point cannot be too strongly emphasised and I wish all of you here to do your utmost to instill into the minds of the people that State property belongs to all of us individually and collectively, and that it is therefore incumbent upon us to do everything in our power to protect such property from unscrupulous persons who may wish to misuse State property for their personal ends.

Now that we are establishing State farms, State factories, State corporations and other organisations of State, in order to secure our economic future, neglect towards State property could spell disaster for the national economy.

I hope that during your group discussions you will be able to formulate plans and programmes which will strengthen the forward move of our Party, avoiding any conflict between the Party and the people.

Let us always remember that the strength of the Government depends upon the unity and solidarity of the Party and its faithful and unflinching support of the masses, and that in the final analysis, the strength of the Party depends upon the honesty, sincerity and loyalty of the individual members who compose it.

And now, Comrades, I consider that I have spoken long enough to give you some idea of the work and task that this Seminar hopes to achieve at this Institute, and I must conclude to allow you to give active thought to the various subjects which I have spoken to you about. Good luck!

APPENDIX

SUMMARY OF COMMENTS BY DISCUSSION GROUPS

Party Education

The Groups agreed with Osagyefo's view and emphasised that Party education must go down to the masses at Ward and branch level.

It was suggested that separate educational units by the integral organisations of the Party should be abolished and all organisations of education centralised at the Kwame Nkrumah Institute of Ideological Studies at Winneba.

Groups were of opinion that the Bureau of Party Education should publish Party literature both in English and in the Ghanaian languages. Osagyefo's seminar address, it was suggested, should be published likewise. The Bureau of Party Education should recommend books to wards and branches for serious study.

Party Ideology

The groups stressed that Nkrumah as a philosophy, should be standardised and therefore Central Committee should set up a small committee to produce an approval outline work. The groups suggested that Nkrumaism must be taught officially in all schools, so this committee should be set up as quickly as possible to do this work which should be a guide to teachers and students alike.

Party Rallies

The groups endorsed the suggestion that Party rallies must now take a different look. Speakers and subjects should be properly arranged. Errors and mis-statements at a rally by one speaker should be corrected by the Principal speaker or the Chairman of the rally. Other views expressed by Osagyefo in his address on this topic were wholly supported.

Human Relations

Osagyefo's views were strongly supported by the various groups and emphasis was placed on the need for mutual respect at all levels.

Uniform

The suggestion to put State Construction Workers and other categories of worker into uniform to create confidence and self-respect was enthusiastically received by all groups.

Rumour Mongering, Character Assassination, etc.

All groups vehemently denounced these malpractices and serve measures to be adopted in stamping them out. Very strong support was expressed for Osagyefo under this head and it was suggested that offenders must be punished and disciplined without mercy.

Groups suggested that Disciplinary Committees be set up at Regional and District levels to look into complaints in the first instance before these were sent to National Headquarters.

Village Committees

All groups enthusiastically hailed Osagyefo's idea on this subject. The groups suggested with much emphasis that Government should ensure that these committees were set up, no obstacles were allowed to obstruct their efficient running.

State Properties

Osagyefo's views received a rousing support on this issue. Groups called for appropriate legislation in this regard.

Other Matters

Arising out of their discussions, groups made some useful suggestions covering many aspects of Party organisation and national reconstruction. The following were some of the aspects covered.

(a) **Youth Organisation**

The groups stressed that all youth organisations in the country should be brought under the effective control of the Ghana Young Pioneers in order to ensure the proper national orientation of the Ghanaian youth.

(b) **Designation of Office**

It was suggested by some groups that the title "General Secretary", now employed to designate the office of the Secretaries of the integral organisations of the Party like the T. U. C. and U. G. F. C. should be abolished and the title "Secretary" substituted there for. This would achieved the result that only the General secretary of the Party would be so referred to.

(c) **Committee on Workers Organisation**

The suggestion was put forward that the C.W.O. should be re-introduced to co-ordinate the activities not only of trade unions but also of all integral organisations of the Party. This would ensure the proper behaviour of the Party wings.

(d) **Visit to Regions by Osagyefo**

The groups remarked that Osagyefo's visit to the Regions were most important in giving inspiration to the people so Osagyefo might consider the advisability of undertaking such visits when convenient.

3

GATEWAY TO GHANA

OFFICIAL OPENING OF TEMA HARBOUR

Tema
February 10, 1962

LADIES AND GENTLEMEN,

It is a happy coincidence that the formal opening of Tema harbour, which is destined to be the new industrial gateway to Ghana, should take place so soon after the completion of the negotiations and the inauguration of the Volta River Project. In a sense, of course, the construction of Tema harbour is a part of that project. From the very beginning we realised that if an aluminium industry, such as we envisaged, was to be established, it would require the provision of a modern port which was conveniently situated to serve not only the needs of the Volta River Project, but also the growing and varied needs of the economy of Ghana generally.

Takoradi harbour, which was opened in 1928, has until now been the main port of Ghana, but in spite of extensions that have been made to it, it is still difficult for it to cope speedily and efficiently with the ever increasing volume of trade. What has been needed for several years, is a second deep-water port to handle heavy cargoes which are destined for the eastern part of the country. This new port of Tema, therefore, will not only be able to relieve the congestion of traffic at Takoradi, but also assist greatly in the rapid distribution of imports.

From time immemorial, a great proportion of our imports and exports have been handled at Accra, and at other places along our shores, by he surf boats. The time is fast approaching when this picturesque but hazardous method of handling our cargoes will become a thing of the past. It is important, however that this traditional and vital period of our history should be preserved: preserved not as some carved monument gathering dust in a museum, but as a living tribute to the outstanding skill and courage of our boat boys and the part they have played in our economic development. As soon as Accra harbour ceases to function, therefore, I propose to convert the whole of that area into a pleasure and recreation centre with every amenity for enjoyment and relaxation. I propose moreover that a regatta be held once or twice a year, and that boat races and other water sports are held, when silver cups and other trophies will be completed for.

Ladies and Gentleman: Let me assure you of one thing: Dreams *can* come true!

Ten years ago I wandered about here along with my driver one evening, thinking and planning, dreaming and hoping. Life was not so easy then; for instance there were no roads near here and I had to do a considerable amount of walking to reach where I wanted to be. I remember that evening so clearly. It was the sort of evening, infact, that could not fail to inspire one; the sea lapped lazily against the rocks, a cool but gentle breeze was blowing and the sun was setting in the west with a flush of fiery red.

So real was the harbour that I built around myself that time that evening, that I imagined I could hear the screams of the winches, the sirens of ships, the clammer and chatter of men at work, and the shunting of trains. But I had one problem. Should my baby be born in Tema or Ada? It turned out to be an event bigger problem than I had first envisaged, because I hadn't reckoned with Nii Ocansey and his delegation of Party members from Ada! They too had visions and one day when I attended a function in this area, I was met by a sea of placards which read: "Ada Harbour". Even the seat that I was shown to had "ADA HARBOUR" written across it. Well, although Nii Ocansey and his followers didn't get the harbour, at least they brought things to a head. I realised that I had to make a great political decision and I decided that the Government must act and act immediately.

Ada lost the harbour because if the sit and sand banks which according to the experts, would have necessitated fulltime dredging. But Ada must not think that she has been passed over. Those sand banks are gong to become a veritable paradise on earth. About two months ago I paid a visit to these little island, travelling from the mainland by launch. Even in their natural state they are as beautiful as anything I have yet seen, and I was immediately alerted as to their potential as holiday resorts, places where people will retreat to from all corners of the earth in order to get "away from it all." Ada, in fact, has been re-discovered.

And so it came about that in 1951 we embarked on what is probably the most ambitious harbour project yet to have been undertaken in Africa—the building of this new port and town of Tema.

In order to get some idea of the magnitude of this whole operation, I would like to mention that the town of Tema will eventually consist of twelve communities with a population of about a quarter million people. At the present moment there are only two communities here. As regards the harbour, its capacity will eventually be increased to twenty berths or more, with five quays. We intend to extend and expand the present dry dock (which is capable of taking only small craft, fishing vessels and other minor boats) and bring it to a stage which will make it suitable for taking large merchant and naval ship for repair purposes and also as a ship-building yard. A new fishing harbour is also planned which will be twice the size of the one we have now. In the meanwhile, however, a solid foundation has been provided on which the economic progress of the country can be securely based.

The total cost of the main harbour works up to the present stage of development, amount to some £G27 million, every penny of which has been found from our own resources.

At this point, I would like to refer briefly to the progress we have made in shipping, civil aviation and communications generally in Ghana. The high standards we have maintained in the construction of trunk roads throughout the country have earned us a good reputation on all sides. But on the sea and in the air, the black Star Line and Ghana Airways have proudly taken their places with the services of other nations. The Black Star Line now operates a fleet of thirteen vessels, seven of which are owned by the state. Five new ships are expected to be delivered to us before the end of this year, by which time the total deadweight tonnage of Ghana's mercantile marine will exceed one hundred thousand tons. This is not a bad beginning. And it is interesting to note that all this has been built up within the last three and a half years.

As far as commercial fights are concerned, Ghana now has an impressive fleet of twenty aircraft flying throughout Europe and Africa, and it is their policy to extended their fights to all African states and beyond. And there again it is interesting to note that all these things have been done in the last three and a half years.

We have every reason to hope that this harbour will prove to be a profitable concern and that the shipping of all nations–from the East and from the West–will be attracted here. In particular we offer a special welcome to shipping from our neighbouring and other African states. Indeed, I hope that Tema harbour can become a "free port" for those African states who want to used it. With regard to the handling of cargo in Tema harbour, I would like to mention the fact that the Government has established the Ghana Cargo and Handling Company under the management of W. Biney and Company, whose main purpose is to carry out stevedoring, master porterage and lightering.

We believe that over-all economic planning on a continental basis is an inescapable necessity for the advancement of Africa. I am convinced that we, the independent states of Africa, should now be thinking seriously of ways and means of building up a Common Market of a United Africa, rather than allow ourselves to be lured by the dubious advantages of the European Common Market.

Africa has for too long looked outward for the development of its economy, transportation and even for its arts and culture. From now on, Africa must look inwards into the African continent for all aspects of its development. Our communications in the past have stretched outwards to Europe and elsewhere, instead of developing internally, between our cities and states. All this must be changed. We realise hat it is only by our own exertions that we can bring progress, unity and strength into Africa.

It is our hope that this port which we are opening to-day, will play a useful role in opening up this part of Africa. Many parts of West Africa (and I use West Africa merely as an example to stress the need for continental panning) are very far from the sea. West Africa is not endowed with many natural harbours and the cost of building and artificial harbour is prohibitive for many states. Yet, by concerted action we can build international highways which will connect Tema to other capitals beyond the boundaries of Ghana. It would consequently be possible for other towns outside Ghana to share in the advantages of a modern sea port. By taking advantage of the river systems of West Africa, it should be possible—again, by concerted action—to connect the hinterland, far outside the borders of Ghana, with this great port of Tema. Thus, in this harbour of Tema, we see a unifying force and an essential requirement in the progress towards African unity.

If you look at the map of Ghana to-day, you will find that the road and railway systems were designed by the colonialists to facilitate the exportation of the wealth of the country. This is an essential characteristic of a colonial economy. Since 1951, we in Ghana have endeavoured to break away from this colonial economy. Roads have been built not only to maintain essential exports but to open up the country so that a thriving economy may be generated within the country. Takoradi harbour, although it has been of great benefit to the country, was conceived in the interest of a colonial economy. The vision which created Tema is entirely different. Tema is the sign post of the future. It represents the purposeful beginning of the industrialisation of Ghana. It is the signal for industrial expansion, a challenge to our industry and intelligence and a hope for the future.

Ladies and Gentleman: before I declare this harbour open, I should like to pay tribute to the consulting engineers, Sir William Halcrow and Partners, and to the contractors, Messrs. Parkinson Howard Limited, and to all the many people, both Ghanaian and non-Ghanaian, who have played a part in making Tema harbour what it is to-day. In this connection I would particularly like to mention the valuable service rendered by Sir Eric Milburn, how I am glad to see is with us to-day.

And now, it is my pleasure to declare Tema harbour officially open, and to unveil this commemorative plaque.

4

OPENING OF THE CANADIAN TRADE FAIR

February 14, 1962

Ladies and Gentlemen,

Barely three months ago, we witnessed in Accra the very successful trade exhibition and small industries fair organised by the States Government. Within this same period, we have seen several exhibitions of a similar kind by various governments, including those of the Peoples Republic of China, the Peoples Republic of Yugoslavia, and recently the Federal Republic of Germany.

I am pleased to have been invited by the Canadian High Commissioner to participate in the opening ceremony of this trade exhibition, which is the first of its kind to be held by the Canadian Government in West Africa.

Such exhibitions, are of the utmost importance, and help to stimulate our interest in the economic development taking place in other parts of the world. The fact that many governments have arranged to hold trade shows here, is a clear manifestation of the interest and goodwill which is shown in Ghana by our friends abroad who are ready trio give us the necessary assistance in the economic, industrial and technical development of our country.

It is particularly significant that Canada should by holding a trade exhibition in Ghana. Indeed one way well ask why such an exhibition has not been held earlier. The ties of friendship between Canada and Ghana are very strong. I recall with pleasure the first time I met the Canadian Prime Minister, Mr. Diefenbaker. It was in 1957 at the meeting of Commonwealth Prime Ministers in London. Both of us were attending for the first time. The administration that I had for Mr. Diefenbaker at that time of our first meeting has never waned.

When I visited Canada in 1958, I was highly impressed with the obvious signs of industrial development that I saw. I was privileged to address the members of the Canadian Senate and House of Commons on 21st July, 1958, and I spoke then of the generous assistance we had received from Canada in a number of economic, social and cultural fields. The government of Canada has continued to make notable contributions to our economic development, by providing experts, advisers and training facilities under technical assistance schemes. I should like to take this opportunity to say how grateful we, the government and people of Ghana, are for this assistance.

Our trade and economic relations with Canada have remained very satisfactory. Canada is our chief supplier of wheat flour. In addition, we obtain from her fair quantities of rice, milk and other dairy products. We have reorganised our import control system recently in order to safe-guard and improve our balance of payments position with the rest of the world. I am told that the effect of this reorganisation on our trade with Canada has been negligible. I am confident, therefore, that this exhibition which we are opening today, will result in the further development of the satisfactory trade and economic relations between our two countries, and also strengthen the ties of friendship which already exist between us.

The Commonwealth to which we belong, consists today of different races with different creeds, different forms of government, cultures and background. We regard the Commonwealth as an association of free and independent sovereign states, equal in all respects and bound together by the common desire to work for the good and well being of its members.

We in Ghana are now engaged on producing a new seven-year plan of socio-economic, industrial, agricultural and technological development. We are confident that the new plan, when it comes to be implemented, will stimulate and enhance Ghana's economy and raise it to new heights of productivity and strength. We are however faced with another problem: the dangers to which we are exposed by the prospect of the European Common Market, not only as members of the Commonwealth but particularly as members of the African community.

The policy of the Ghana Government in this matter has been made unmistakably clear. We are opposed to any groupings or arrangements which are used as a cloak for perpetuating colonial privileges in Africa. The unpleasant effect on the Commonwealth of Britain joining the European Common Market cannot be over stead and I am glad that in this matter Canada, like Ghana, is very much alive to the serious issues involved.

We must so plan our economies that we in Africa are nit reduced perpetually to the role of producers of raw materials only. We cannot improve our standard of living by remaining agricultural areas indefinitely, nor can we improve the skill and ingenuity of our peoples by keeping them solely as workers in rural area. This is why we are working so hard and so fast to ensure that the industrial, agricultural and technological development gets started in Ghana right now. Last week we heard the good news that the final documents regarding the financing of the Volta River Project have been signed with the World Bank in Washington. Everything is now ready therefore for work on this great project to begin in earnest. From now on there can be no turning back and we look forward to the day when there will be enough electric power throughout the towns and villages of Ghana, to sustain our industrial activity.

I am glad to mention here with the assistance of the Canadian Prime Minister Mr. Diefenbaker himself, we have been able to recruit for the important job of chief executive of the Volta River Authority, Mr. Dobson, an experienced Canadian engineer.

Ladies and Gentlemen; once again, I would like to welcome this exhibition to Ghana and to express the hope that it will strengthen the relations between Canada and the Republic of Ghana.

It is with great pleasure therefore that I declare the Canadian Trade Exhibition open.

5

AFRICA NEEDS HER FARMERS

THE CONFERENCE OF
THE FARMERS OF AFRICA

Legon
March 19, 1962

Mr. Chairman, Respected Delegates and Friends,

I am happy to be with you this morning and to have the opportunity to bid the distinguished delegates welcome to Ghana. For the first time in history, African farmers and peasants from all parts of our great-continent are meeting here in Accra, to discuss and deliberate upon the welfare of farmers and peasants, and upon the progress and prosperity of Africa.

The importance of agriculture in the African economy and, consequently, the vital role of farmers and peasants in the general economic reconstruction and the rehabilitation of our people after years of colonial devastation and ravages, cannot be over emphasised.

As I see it, your major task is the creation of a complete revolution in agriculture on our continent—a total break with primitive methods and organisations with the colonial past which tied the African down to subsistence farming, cultivated monocultural crops all over the continent, created scarcity in the midst of abundance and kept our masses at a very low ebb of nutritional and sub-economic standards.

Now that we are our own masters and now that the end of colonialism in Africa has become a fact, the world would show us little sympathy if we made no endeavour to do our own planning to mechanise and diversify our agriculture and introduce new forms, ways and methods to revitalise our farming society.

There must be a new African farmer who understands the needs of the new Africa and who looks beyond the limits of his own requirements. He must be imbued with a keen sense of pan-African nationalism and determination to banish hunger not only from his own territory or state, but from the whole of Africa.

This is a mighty undertaking which can only be achieved by united effort. Agriculture must not merely provide food for our people; it must create industrial strength by providing raw materials both for exports and for home manufacture.

The new hold on Africa by neo-colonialism, which is fighting desperately to control our very existence and development, must be shattered. But our only hope of succeeding in this is by a united mutual effort. That is why we must constantly think, speak and work towards African unity. Whether it comes to-day, tomorrow or the day after, it must come if Africa is to survive.

As I said sometime ago, enemies of African progress and prosperity have a vested interest in misinterpreting our motives in order to confuse African nationalist leaders on this question of African unity. The fact that farmers and peasants of so many African countries have, by their own initiative and free will, gathered together here to-day with the idea of forming a united continental organisation which would advance your interest and cater for the welfare of Africa as a whole, is incontestible proof of your belief in African unity as being the only means to our future. Similarly, African trade unionists have already noted the urgent necessity for coming together and have formed the All African Trades Union Federation. These and other examples of unity in some aspects of our African activity point clearly and unmistakably to the overriding necessity for African unity.

The political and economic unification of the African continent is the key—the master key—to Africa's future.

It is natural that each one of us should be proud of his own states, its national flag and national anthem. We of this generation shall never forget the price that we had to pay in order to hoist that flag and to sing that national anthem in our own free and independent territory, even though the barriers between their territories are artificial and not of our own making. Those who come after us will read about it in their history books, will share our pride, will applaud some of our actions and criticise others.

By all means let us respect each other's sovereignty and independence, let us fly with love and pride our national flags and sing with joy and thankfulness our national anthems. But we cannot afford to be smug and we cannot blind ourselves to the liability side of our balance sheets—the cost of keeping our flags flying.

Socially, economically and culturally we are interconnected. None of us, for instance, is economically independent. As things stands, three possibilities are upon to us: to look to each other and pool our resources, to look to one or other of the foreign powers and become dependent upon them, or to isolate ourselves and regress. There can be no question in the mind of any African that a overall economic industrial and agricultural planning on a united continental basis would increase the industrial and economic power of Africa. But this cannot be achieved until we come together in a political union to give political direction.

Then there is the question of our armed forces. Here we are, in our independent states, spending millions a year to train and equip our men for our defence forces. But if the worst came to the worst, what chance would our armies have, standing alone, individually, against he force and might of most foreign armies to-day? How much more sensible and realistic it would be if we formed a joint military command, an African army an African navy and an African air force. Not only would such a force be effective and equal in strength and efficiency to any other in the world, but the cost of maintaining it, compared to what we are each paying for our individual armed forces at the moment, would be infinitesimal.

And apart from this aspect of it, if we do not unite and combine our military forces for common defence, some African states, out of a sense of insecurity, may be drawn individually into making defence pacts with foreign powers which will endanger the unity and security of our continent.

If we set up a common economic planning organisation and joint military command, then we must also adopt a common foreign policy and a common diplomatic representation abroad. How will our small and young states, for instance, find the resources to staff embassies in the independent States of Africa, let alone foreign countries abroad? The financial burden will be great and the people will be the sufferers.

It should be possible for us to devise some constitutional structure which preserves the sovereignty of each state and at the same time make it possible for us to have a political union on common economic and agricultural planning, a common army, navy and air force and a common foreign policy and diplomacy. I envisage that countries in such a union will maintain their own constitutions, continue to use their own national flags, their national anthems and other national symbols and paraphernalia of sovereignty. No union states need surrender any of these things. Yet when we speak of political union, and decry the balkanisation of Africa, detractors and enemies of Africa are quick to observe and attempt on our part to impose leadership and abrogate sovereignty. They use this as a screen to hide their deep fear of African unity. They would stop at nothing to undermine its attainment.

Mr. Chairman and Delegates: Africa's salvation lies in a continental national union and we who have the responsibility of leading the people must hurry and come together, if we are to prevent the catastrophic devastation of our continent by the activities of neo-colonialists.

Mr. Chairman and Delegates, by noon today the cease-fire agreement signed between the Algerian Provisional Government and French authorities at Evian will come into force. With this comes to an end the seven-year struggle of the Algerian people for peace and independence. We welcome the cease-fire agreement as a basis for the total emancipation of Algeria. The struggle has been long and bitter, but it has given the Algerian people the right to govern themselves, and place Algeria in a position to march fully with us in our struggle for the freedom and unity of Africa.

We salute our brothers in Algeria today and wish them well in the years that lie ahead.

And now Mr. Chairman, I have great pleasure in declaring open this Conference of All African Farmers' Organisations. I wish it every success, and hope you will feel at home and fully enjoy your short stay here with us.

6

GHANA WELCOMES FOREIGN ENTERPRISE

AT THE CIVIC LUNCHEON

**Kumasi,
March 24, 1962**

LADIES AND GENTLEMEN,

I am grateful for the address of welcome which has just been presented to me. I also thank you for this fine reception, and the many expressions of loyalty and confidence in the Party and Government which have been made.

I have listened with great interest to the history of this Municipality which has been recounted. The improvements and the development projects which have taken place in Kumasi in recent years, represent a magnificent record, and bear testimony to the dynamism of our great Party.

Everybody knows of the horrible atrocities and treacherous manoeuvres which took place in Kumasi and in many parts of Ashanti before, and even after, our independence. You, Mr. Chairman, have declared in your address that there has been a change of heart in Ashanti. I accept this assurance. Indeed, the fact that I have come here to-day to declare Kumasi a City should be sufficient confirmation that the Party and the Government recognise this change of heart.

But Mr. Chairman and friends, at a time like this, when Kumasi assumes the great responsibility of a new and higher status, it is of the utmost importance that we should all place our cards on the table face upwards, and do some plain speaking on matters that might operate to obstruct the success not only of this new city but indeed of the country as a whole.

I must say that I personally am disturbed by certain tendencies on the part of some Party comrades and councillors. Here in Ashanti, and to some extent, in other parts of the country, matters relating to chieftaincy are causing a great deal of unrest and strife in our Party. This is an unfortunate position and must be corrected promptly.

Here and there a chief's stool becomes vacant. Two Party comrades contest for enstoolment. One succeeds. Immediately the loser of the stool contest becomes aggrieved and turns against the Party and Government. Not only that, he at once sets out to undermine the successful comrade who has been enstooled. Both of them have supporters on their sides so unnecessary strife ensure and the Party splits over this issue of chieftaincy.

In future the Party and Government will take a very serious view of such matters and adopt very drastic measures to correct this state of affairs in our towns and villages. Government will for instance quickly remove any person from a traditional area who indulges in such disruptive activities and thereby tends to undermine not only the progress and prosperity of the villages and towns but also the solidarity of the Party.

Reference to Party solidarity brings to my mind the question of admission of new members into the Party. The Central Committee directed some time ago that all persons shall be admitted to the Party irrespective of their political past, provided that such persons accept the Party ideology and policies and programme.

In spite of this directive, many comrades resent and object to the admission of new entrants either out of sheer vindictiveness or out of ignorant jealousy. I must emphasise the point that the Party is supreme and will be supreme in all ways always.

No one can remain a Party member and defy Party directives issued by the Central Committee. Henceforth, therefore, any Party member or members who obstruct the admission of ex-members of the defunct United Party seeking admission into our great Party will be dealt with in a fitting manner. We cannot talk loudly of building a one-Party state and yet drive away persons who would want to join the Party and help to realise that objective. Furthermore no money should be collected from newcomers. Party officials, District Commissioners and all who deal with Party membership must bear this in mind and guide themselves accordingly. Let me leave no doubt in the minds of all concerned that those who disobey this directive will only have themselves to blame.

Let me now turn my attention to councillors. Very often, I wonder whether councillors understand their duties and responsibilities. Many councillors all over the country easily forget that in point of fact, they are servants of the people. They grow a sense of over-importance and become arrogant and oppressive in their attitude to the people who elected them to the council. Indeed it is true to say that councillors are tending to become a class unto themselves.

I want to lay stress on the fact that we are working to build a socialist state and that the Party cannot stand by and allow this baneful conduct to develop. We are protectors of the masses and I personally will not tolerate any position in which the ordinary person in this Ghana is scorned and made a footstool. Councillors are servants not, master of the people.

I thought that the recent action taken by Party and Government to discipline all comrades starting from the top, that is to say, with Ministers and Deputy Ministers, ought to be an eye opener to all of us. This, however, has not been the case. Some councillors think that it is fashionable to be dishonest and they play funny tricks of all sorts with council contracts. Some even, who are contractors conceal this fact instead of declaring their interests when dealing with council contracts.

This is most disgusting and in future really drastic steps will be taken against any councillor found guilty of such conduct. The ten per cent commissions extorted from contractors in the name of the Party must stop and stop for good.

I have stated over and over again that public office must not be used for personal gain. Public service demands honesty, devotion and integrity and I am again warning all councillors to eschew all forms of corruption and advance the interests and well-being of the masses of our people from whom the Party derives its strength.

The Party applies one discipline to all its members—we do not and cannot have different corrections for different persons in respect of an identical offence. Everyone of us is subject to the authority of the

Party treats all members the same. In this regard, I shall cause councillors to be investigated in the same manner as I did with Ministers, etc., and even though in the case of councillors their office is not paid office, still they are members of our great Party, they have taken oath to serve the people faithfully and honestly and they must remain true to that oath and keep faith with the people.

Mr. Chairman and friends, we know precisely what goes on in these councils and we must do everything to eliminate the evils that militate against our Party and our national interests. The Party, from now on, will exercise greater control on Party councillors who must accept this whip or resign.

A new pattern of councils will be adopted which will enable all constituencies to be turned into districts and all districts, unlike at present, will have their own local councils with their own district commissioners. This will facilitate council work and administration and, make for greater efficiency.

I have directed also that local dialects must be used in their deliberations. This measure will surely allow the election to the council of men and women who do not read and write English. This, I hope, should bring new blood of native wisdom of our fathers and mothers to local councils and improve the quality of their integrity. Traditional councils on the other hand, must continue to group themselves into larger units.

In order to make administration at the base as effective as possible the Party and Government intend to introduce village committees all over the country. A village committee will comprise the chairman of the local Party branch and small number of other comrades in whom administrative responsibility of the village, however small, would be vested by law.

I now come to an important matter—the question of detention. Government will amend the Preventive Detention Act so that release after five years ceases to be automatic as at present. Now, when a person is detained, Government will decide at the end of five years whether he should be released or not. If a detainee is released and continues the conduct which first sent him to detention, he will be detained again but this time for twenty years.

Legislation will also soon be introduced to protect state property. Hitherto we have trifled with must state property with impunity. The position will change. The law will be so made that anyone found guilty of stealing, damaging or in any way at all interfering with State property will be liable to the severest punishment possible.

As I have said before elsewhere, the paramount task before us and the nation, is the establishment of an equitable and progressive social order which will provide food, clothing and shelter to met the need of the people, in accordance with their means; a social order which will bring to the mass of the people, happiness and a higher standard of living. This means the attainment of full employment, the provision of good housing, and equal opportunity for educational and cultural advancement for all the people.

This is a task in which the Municipal Councils like the Kumasi Council, and all local authorities, can be of positive assistance. It cannot be left to the Party and Government alone. City, Municipal and Local Councils, all Local Authorities, must be prepared to assume responsibilities for initiating and implementing local plans within the framework of our national policy. Local Authorities can be of great assistance, for example, in helping to solve the problem of boys and girls who gravitate to Accra and other big towns in search of jobs which do not exist. Local Authorities ought to be addressing themselves to problems of this nature, which they alone experience intimately.

It is for this reason that chairmen of City and Municipal Councils have recently been appointed to serve on the Regional Administrative Committees of which Regional Commissioners are chairmen. For efficient administration, traditional areas will remain as they are, but each District will be administered exclusively by a District Commissioner. District Commissioners, moreover, will all be of equal status.

In order that Chairmen of City and Municipal Councils may be enabled to devote full attention to their duties and to carry them out more efficiently, I have reviewed the emoluments which are granted to the holders of this important post. I have directed that as from the 1st March, 1962, all chairmen of Municipal and City Councils should be paid a salary of one thousand eight hundred pounds a year plus an entertainment allowance of two hundred and fifty pounds a year. In addition, chairmen of Municipal and City Councils will be entitled to free bungalow accommodation.

In the past, Chairmen of Municipal Councils have paid visits to neighbouring West African territories, and have also received delegations from those countries. Serious consideration should be given to the convening in the near future of a conference of African Local Authorities at which mutual problems can be discussed. In this way, you will be playing your part in the march towards African unity. We must begin to think in terms of African continental planning and development.

Mr. Chairman, I would like to thank you for the magnificent gifts which have been given to me and Madam Fathia by the Municipal Council. We will treasure them as a memento of this historic occasion.

And now, it gives me great pleasure to declare formally the elevation of Kumasi to the honourable status of a City. I am confident that the Council and the citizens of this City will prove themselves worthy of the high honour and distinction conferred on them to-day.

7

THE LAYING OF THE FOUNDATION STONE OF CITY HOTEL

Kumasi
March 24, 1962

LADIES AND GENTLEMEN,

A few hours ago, I formally conferred the status of a City on the Municipality of Kumasi. And now, we are met here this afternoon to lay the foundation stone of the first modern and up-to-date hotel in this Region. The Hotel Industry in Ghana is a new development in the social and economic life of our country. Many of you here will remember the serious opposition we had to face when it was decided to build the Ambassador Hotel in Accra. The sceptics among us declared that the project was a waste of valuable funds; others said the hotel would prove to be a white elephant and that it would never pay its way. Nevertheless, the Government went ahead with the hotel project because we were then, as now devoted to the economic, industrial and technological progress of Ghana and her people. The results of our initiative, needless to say, have belied all the gloomy forebodings made at the that time and some of our severest critics have become the most regular and enthusiastic patrons of the Ambassador Hotel!

It is the aim of the Party and Government to establish a chain of first class hotels throughout the country, because we believe that the services which hotels provides represent an important contribution to the general development and industrialisation of Ghana.

The building of this hotel in Kumasi is a continuation of the policy which we have followed all along. We are shortly to form a Ghana Hotels Corporation which will be responsible for the establishment and organisation of hotels throughout the country. This Corporation will work hand in hand with the Ghana Holiday and Tourist Agency which has recently been established so as to make the best use of the tourist facilities available in the country.

Kumasi has, from its earliest days, been an important meeting place of the road and rail systems if Ghana and, as such, it has come to be used as a travellers' rest. In this age of jet and space travel, however, when visitors are liable to drop in to see us from places as far removed from one another as Timbuktu and Tokyo, Kano and Moscow, Ouagadougou and New York, the time has come to build a modern hotel in this traditional crossroads city to accommodate these visitors in a fitting manner, and in keeping with our traditional hospitality.

Kumasi with its rich cultural heritage, its great forest and natural beauty spots, will always be an attraction for visitors. But in addition to holiday-makers and sightseers, with the rapid development of commerce and industry, not only between the African States, but between Africa and the territories outside our continent, the demand for hotel accommodation by businessmen and trade delegates will continue to increase. This new hotel therefore represents an essential development of the age in which we live.

In recent years Kumasi and the Ashanti Region have played a distinctive role in Ghana's economic and industrial expansion. Many of our industrial projects have been sited here. The manufacture of biscuits and beer, two popular products, are undertaken by enterprising factories in Kumasi. Timber products have for a long time reflected the richness of Ashanti forests. A new and important industry which is being built up in this Region is the jute factory that will produce more than four million cocoa bags a year, and thus put an end to the perennial shortage of cocoa bags which our farmers have to face during the peak periods of production in the cocoa season.

In planning our industrial expansion, more and more emphasis will be placed on developing rural industries in such a way that factories can be planned as near to the available raw materials as possible, and so give the same opportunities for employment to the people who live in the rural areas as in the big towns. So great has been the pace of development in Ghana, that our five-year plan has had to be abandoned, because it failed to meet our urgent needs and aspirations. We are now engaged in preparing a new and comprehensive seven-year plan for the economic, industrial, agricultural and technological development of the country. We hope to inaugurate this plan in January, 1963. Thus by 1970, the completion of the plan will coincide with tenth anniversary of our Republic.

May I now draw your attention to an important matter. The direct participation of the Government in industry appears to have created doubts about Government's intentions in regard to the part that can be played by overseas capital and investments in the development of Ghana.

With the conclusion of the Volta Loan Agreement, the Government has received a large number of enquiries from business and finance interests from overseas which demonstrate keenness to participate, to an increasing degree, in the development of the country's economy. It is appropriate therefore, that I should take this opportunity to re-define the Government's policy in regard to private enterprise and investment in general.

It is the declared policy of the Government to build a society in which the principles of social justice will be paramount. Towards this end it will maintain its policy of economic planning and increasing participation in the nation's economic activity.

We have decided, therefore, that in no sector of the economy will exclusive rights of operation in respect of any commodity be conferred on any single person, company or establishment; all enterprises are expected to accept the economic policy of the Government as the basis of their activity and to operate within the framework of the laws of the nation.

The Government recognises five sectors, all operating side by side in the nation's economy. These sectors are:-

1. *State enterprises.*
2. *Enterprises owned by foreign interests.*
3. *Enterprises jointly owned by the State and foreign private interests.*
4. *Co-operatives.*
5. *Small-scale Ghanaian private enterprises.*

State enterprises are the enterprises completely owned and operated by the State, and will include all enterprises managed under the direction of the competent governmental organs.

Firstly, to ensure an evergrowing and steady employment for the people, secondly, to increase national income and the revenues of the State in order to raise the living standards of the people, to expend and improve both education and health services.

Thirdly, to have at the command of the State significant and growing stocks of commodities in order to be able to influence the market, this influence being aimed at the stabilization of the price level and that of currency. Lastly, to supply those services, which the private sector does not wish or is not allowed to supply.

The Government accepts the operation in the country of large-scale enterprises by foreign interests, provided that they accept the following conditions: firstly that foreign private enterprises give the Government the first option to buy their shares, whenever it is intended to sell all or part of the equity capital; and secondly that foreign private enterprises and enterprises jointly owned by the state and foreign private interests be required to re-invest 60 per cent of their net profits in Ghana.

Enterprises jointly owned by the state and foreign private interests will be operated jointly by Government and private foreign interests, whose respective shares in the equity capital shall be agreed by both parties.

Government will support and encourage the formation of co-operative enterprises of producers both in agriculture, as well as in trade and industry.

In order to encourage and utilize personal initiative and skill, Ghanaians can undertake small-scale enterprises, provided that they are not nominees or sleeping partners of foreign interests.

In future the private small-scale personal enterprise sector will be exclusively reserved for the Ghanaians. Foreign concerns already established in this sector will be allowed to continue operation, in condition that they do not expand their present establishment, and scale of operations. In future, therefore, there will be no room for overseas interests in the small-scale enterprises sector in Ghana.

Our aim is to build up Ghana into a strong and progressive nation, economically, industrially and technologically, and foreign private interests are invited to share in this development.

We want to see that every citizen of Ghana has the opportunity to develop his or her abilities to the fullest extent, in order to make maximum contribution to the country's development. We must realise, that the strength and character of a nation depends on the quality of its citizens. It must be our aim, therefore, to build a State which will be universally acknowledged as honest and incorruptible. The state organisations and factories which we are daily establishing represent a great challenge to the energy and integrity of our people: whether they are in direct charge of such organisations, or whether they are ordinary employees in the enterprises.

If we are to succeed as a nation, every single one of us must be dedicated to the service of the State, and our fellow men. Our State enterprises such as this Hotel, will provide employment of a very responsible nature, to many Ghanaians. The State is entitled to expect loyalty, honest, integrity and good service from all those who will be employed in it. This is the least that we can expect.

The State is however entitled to more than this: it requires maximum dedication to its service. The abuse of power, through dishonesty, is an abomination and should not be tolerated. The misuse of office for selfish ends is a crime against the Party and the State, and it will be treated as such, and dealt with accordingly.

In initiating the construction of this Hotel, I would like to express the hope that it will, on completion become a vital and valuable link in the long chain of State enterprises which are becoming such a dominant feature of Ghana today, and that it will contribute to the economic and industrial development of our dear country.

Ladies and Gentleman, I now have great pleasure in declaring the foundation stone of the City Hotel well and truly laid.

8
THE NINTH ANNUAL NATIONAL DELEGATES' CONFERENCE

CONFERENCE OF THE UNITED GHANA FARMERS' COUNCIL

Kumasi
March 26, 1962

MR. CHAIRMAN, COMRADE FARMERS,

I salute you all, and congratulate you most heartily on the Ninth Anniversary of the United Ghana Farmers' Council which you are celebrating to-day. I am glad to be with you this morning, as you met in session, to discuss ways and means of providing for the welfare of your Council and its members, and the prosperity of Ghana.

The United Ghana Farmers' Council, which we established in 1953, has fully justified its existence, and has been able to rally the farmers of this country behind the Government, in mutual confidence and understanding.

The problems facing us in the agricultural sector of our economy are numerous and formidable, and the Party and Government expect that you, the farmers of Ghana, will give us every assistance in solving these problems. I am confident that this assistance and support will be readily forthcoming.

Our basic and fundamental need is to increase as rapidly as possible the production and productivity and yield of the agricultural industry. We are now pursuing vigorously a policy of industrialisation, and in a few years time, we can expect to see a growing number of factories and industrial projects throughout the country. This industrial development must, however, be paralleled by increasing productivity in agriculture. For, as productivity increases, the farmer should have an increasing surplus to offer in exchange for manufactured goods. Moreover, as production and productivity grow, the proportion of the population engaged ion food production should fall, thus making labour available for industry. Our plans for industrialisation will therefore depend, to a great degree on the vigour and the productivity of our farming operations throughout the country.

We look to our farmers to provide food in sufficient quantities, for the people to eat. We cannot tolerate the position which exists today regarding the imports of food. The latest statistics show that we are importing every year into Ghana over twenty million pounds worth of food. It has been estimated that if the present rend continues, we shall, by 1970, have to import nearly eight million pounds worth of food to feed the rising population. Food imports amounted to nearly one fifth of all imports into Ghana in 1960. Many of the foodstuffs which are imported could have been produced in Ghana. You will realise therefore that you farmers of Ghana have a great task before you. You must help to stop this unnecessary waste of the country's resources for the benefit of foreign interests. This is a challenge to you.

The Government's agricultural policy is designed to accelerate a break-through in agricultural production, and to provide a sound basis for the establishment of food industries throughout the country. Surveys are being carried out for the establishment of large state farms, and agricultural settlements in various parts of the country. Foreigners who come to Ghana always wonder at the sight of large areas, apparently useful for farming, which are left uncultivated, while the country imports such a large proportion of its food from abroad.

Mr. Chairman and Comrades, we must put to an end as quickly as possible, this sad paradox in our agricultural development. I can see in my mind's eye, vast areas of cultivated farms with mile after mile of produce: corn, cassava, guava, oranges, pineapples and other food crops. That is the type of Ghanaian agriculture we desire. That is the type of agriculture we must and will develop.

There is reason why we should not produce in abundance, and become an exporting country in agriculture foodstuff.

I have recently given directions that all the agricultural stations now run by the Ministry of Agriculture throughout the country should be turned into state farms, and reorganised so as to concentrate more on the production of food for the country.

The United Ghana Farmers' Council has shown in many ways that it can be relied upon by the state to pursue vigorously the duties set before it. When it was decided last year that the Council and its agricultural co-operative bodies should be entrusted with the task of buying the country's cocoa crops, I must confess that I had my misgivings and doubts of your ability to undertake the job. The responsibility was great, and a failure in the enterprise might have spelt disaster for us all. In the face of extreme difficulties, the Council has successfully carried out the operation entrusted to it, and the purchase of the record cocoa has been carried out in a most efficient and orderly manner. I must congratulate the United Ghana Farmers' Council, and all farmers of the country, and all those who assisted in this operation, for this remarkable achievement.

Let me, however, sound a note of warning. You must find ways and means of preventing some dishonest secretary-receivers from defrauding farmers of their cocoa by shortweight. This is a matter which must receive your most serious consideration for some secretary-receivers like to enrich themselves at the expense of the farmer by recording less weight of cocoa for he seller than the actual weight registered by the scale.

Later the secretary-receiver collects the surplus weight from the individual bags of cocoa and he, without owning a cocoa farm, gets cocoa to sell in other people's pocketing the ill-gotten money. This shameful practice must stop for it stains your otherwise unblemished record.

You must also continue to be as vigilant in the future as you have been this year. Do not allow yourselves to be lulled into a false sense of security and optimism. The rules which you adopted in this year for the purchase of cocoa must be improved upon and tightened next year so that the operations will be even more successful in the future.

When in 1959 we launched the Second Five-Year Development Plan, the farmers of Ghana voluntarily agreed to a deduction of twelve shillings per load of 60 lb. from the current cocoa price, and paid the proceeds into the development fund. This was a noble sacrifice, which was appreciated by the whole country. You have recently given another example of your patriotism and devotion to the cause of Ghana's progress by your decision to forgo the deduction of six shillings per load of your cocoa over the next ten years. This act of faith in Ghana, and this positive assistance and contribution to our economic and industrial struggle will not go unrecorded in the history of our times. I take this opportunity, therefore, to express on behalf of the Government and Party my sincere appreciation to the farmers of Ghana for this courageous and generous sacrifice and patriotism which we hope many will be persuaded to emulate.

Recently the Government has enacted legislation which will protect farmers from the exploitation which they have suffered so long. I refer to the Farm Land (Protection) Act and the Rent (Stabilisation) Act. No more will farmers be deprived of their farm because the land on which their farm is situated had been previously acquired by another person. Neither will farmers be forced to pay exorbitant rents for their farming land has now been fixed by law at five shillings per acre per annum.

The imposition of special levy on cocoa by Local Councils or by any organisation or person should be abolished; and if it should be done at all it should be with the consent of farmers in the area.

A week ago, I inaugurated in Accra the Conference of all African Farmers Organisations. It is indeed gratifying to me that the idea I proposed to you in 1960 at your Seventh Annual Conference held at Kpandu, has borne such fruit. I am sure that this All African Union of Farmers which you have launched will become an important link in the chain of African unity. I was so impressed by the effort of the farmers in organising this Conference of unity at Legon.

African farmers have seen the light of unity. So have African Trade Unionists. What about African co-operators? I am sure they also have an obligation and duty to rally themselves in unity and organise themselves into a continental union of African co-operatives in the overall interest of themselves and of African unity. The need for a strong political union of African states is so clear and inescapable that we must bend all our will to ensure its realisation. There is no alternative if we are to survive.

Mr. Chairman, Comrades and Friends: I have great pleasure in declaring this Ninth Annual National Delegates' Conference of the United Ghana Farmers' Council open. I wish your deliberations all success.

9

OPENING OF THE FIRST BIENNIAL CONFERENCE OF THE GHANA T.U.C.

Kumasi
March 26, 1962

MR. CHAIRMAN, COMRADE DELEGATES, LADIES AND GENTLEMEN,

The last time I addressed a convention of the Trades Union Congress was at Cape Coast on the 26th January, 1958. At that time your Congress was re-examining the trade union structure of Ghana and I promised you my full support in the building of a unified trade union movement that will be a true expression of a Ghanaian worker.

Three years have elapsed since that Congress and today I am happy and proud to come amongst you to inaugurate your first biennial convention.

In the name of the Central Committee of the Convention People's Party, I congratulate my fellow trade unionists in the magnificent job you have done in building a new trades union structure, which reflects Ghanaian and African conditions and circumstances.

My own association with the Trade union movement is something which is always of a particular pride to me. I always have a pleasant memory of my membership of the National Maritime Union of America and I like to emphasise the fact that the Convention People's Party of Ghana which I have the honour to lead, is a Party that brings together workers, farmers and peasants, small traders, women and co-operators—in short, all those struggling in a common front to re-organise our society by abolishing the exploitation of man by man.

As I said when opening your Hall of Trade Union in July, 1960, "the convention People's Party under whose protective wing is organised the Trade Union Congress, the United Ghana Farmers' Council, the National Co-operative Council, the National Council of Ghana Women, is committed to fight for a social order in which man is freed from economic exploitation. Every man irrespective of his origin and possession must be free to develop his faculties."

I understand some persons who have not understood the Ghanaian revolution, have raised some doubts as to the correctness of our policy regarding the Trade Union. Our answer to them is: come to Ghana and see things for yourselves.

Our Trade Union branches meet and discuss workers' problems in complete freedom. They elect their own officers and form national unions without any outside interference, and these in turn come together to constitute the Trades Union Congress. The Trade Union Organisations of our country receive instructions from no one except from the workers themselves.

The Ghana T. U. C. enjoys complete freedom of action in deciding matters that affect the welfare of the Ghanaian worker. Freedom, however, does not operate in a vacuum, nor is it irresponsible. Freedom connotes necessity. So our trade unions must relate their freedom of action to the overall needs and welfare of our country. This is in accord with our own way of life and the Party therefore gives guidance to all sections, of our people including workers, farmers and peasants, and co-ordinates our national action in one great united effort for the good of our people. Representatives of the Trade Unions therefore sit in our Central Committee and are part and parcel of the collective leadership of the Party. It is the Central Committee that guides all of us in our journey to Socialist reconstruction.

I have stated these facts so that our detractors can understand what is going on in Ghana. I worked as a steward on board one of the passenger ships of the Clyde Millory Line and I gained practical experience of the value that a good trade union is to its members. In the United Kingdom, I organised coloured workers to combat the exploitation of their labour power. What is more, my whole philosophy of life is Marxian, a fact which ranges me immediately on the side of any organisation fighting to abolish the exploitation of man by man. I have actively encouraged since the beginning of our struggle, the building of a virile and responsible trade union movement because I believe that it is necessary to give correct leadership to the workers for the great exercise of the industrial and economic reconstruction of our country.

The Government which is formed by the Convention People's Party is a people's Government, that is, a worker's, a farmers' and a peasants' Government:—indeed a government of the people—free, strong and independent pursuing a socialist pattern of reconstruction. The interest of workers is therefore will catered for by the State. The trade unions therefore have a different role from that of trade unions in a capitalist society. Indeed the desires and wishes of our working people, farmers and peasants from the basis of our social and economic policy.

I had occasion, while opening the Hall of Trade Union to refer to our programme. We want to see our working people in full employment. There must be jobs for all and we envisage a society in which he who is able but does not work, neither shall he eat. Our educational facilities have been expanded to enable Ghanaian children, whether of workers, farmers or peasants to have equal opportunities for education. Our health services are being improved. All this progress is directed towards improving the living standards and cultural and spiritual needs of our people.

I spoke recently to the nation regarding the Volta River Project and its possibilities of increasing the material wealth of the country—electrification is the to industrialisation. So we must electrify Ghana in order to build up our industries.

Comrades, we have made all these advances because of the co-operation between all sections of our community. But here I must have a serious word of advice to our Trade Union officials. In our present stage of development they must discard their colonial mentality and methods and remember that they are not struggling against capitalists. And where they have to fight against exploiters the state shall be their protector. Today their work must be different. They must spearhead the effort to raise production and productivity and cease to be impeccable advocates for out-moded conditions.

Our trade unions should not limit their activities to the education of workers only as regards their rights, but also regarding their duties and responsibilities. You must inculcate in our working people the love for labour and increased productivity. If the Government is pursuing socialist policies which will be to the ultimate benefit of the workers, the trade unions must assist in explaining these measures to the rank and file instead of becoming mere agitators to rights already protected and guaranteed by the State.

Without our national stability, wealth and security, where will be the rising standards? It is very important therefore that our trade union officials should have a new orientation of their role in this reconstruction exercise. That is why I am happy to note that your Convention is taking place under the slogan "Towards Nkrumaism—the Role and Tasks of the Trade Unions". The new era of trade unionism must come about through increased educational facilities for all trade union branch officials and I have no doubt that the TUC will take full advantage of the courses being offered at the Kwame Nkrumah Ideological Training Institute at Winneba.

Party officials and Trade Union officials must work hand in hand in raising the ideological consciousness of our workers. From the ranks of the workers must come the most devoted and active Party cadres. The trade unions through the Party must educate the new generation of workers entering industry from the rural areas and make them feel at home in their new industrial surroundings.

Apart from the matters I have mentioned which are internal to the Ghana T.U.C., we as a nation today have many responsibilities beyond the borders of our country.

We cannot live here in isolation. We are part and parcel of the total struggle going on in Africa to rid our continent of colonialism in all its forms and manifestations. In this field, the role of Ghana T.U.C. cannot be over emphasised. By your industry and example many workers today who are still languishing under the heels of colonial oppression must have hope soon for liberation.

The workers of Ghana must play their part in achieving African labour unity by building an all African trade union federation. Our role is to help in the struggle to wipe out imperialism, colonialism and neo-colonialism from this continent and to erect in its place a union of free independent African State. The all-African trade union federation must be a vital force in this crusade.

African trade unions, in the march of events, must make their positive contribution to the political unification of Africa through economic integration. But African trade unions can only achieve any worthwhile results if they are free from all entangling affiliations. The Trade Unions of Africa must be free and independent owing allegiance neither to the ICFTU nor to the WFTU nor to any others foreign trade union federation but to co-operate freely and independently with these bodies in the interest of workers everywhere.

African trade unions must federate in a continental union to re-express the African policy of non-alignment. Far from being negative, this policy is positive and establishes a central position which enables co-operation with and fosters unity among all workers of the world.

The trade unions of Africa must not lose sight of their major objective which is the overthrow of colonialism and imperialism and the smashing of colonialist and capitalist exploitation in Africa. However the attitude of a T.U.C. in an independent African State must be distinguished from that of a T.U.C. in a colonial territory. In the former the T.U.C. must mobilise for rapid national economic development and this must dictate the necessity for wage restraint and personal sacrifice on the part of workers for the greatest good of themselves and all the people. In the latter the T.U.C. must be organised for political action: the overthrow of colonialism. This is a vitally important fact for the Ghana T.U.C. to remember pressing question, for the economic balkanisation of Africa must be prevented at all costs.

When African states run helter skelter to outside powers for aid, they surely compromise their independence of thought and action. Imagine therefore the cumulation effect of such action—African states become collectively dependent on outside resources, when they have more than enough resources between themselves, if only they would pool these resources together in conscious unity.

It is good somehow to talk of aid, aid, aid. But is aid all that innocent? Do Africans really believe that they can run after and feel free to exercise their sovereignty with respect and dignity? I have made it clear that as far as Ghana is concerned, we want trade not aid. But if any aid does come to us it must come on our conditions.

In this connection our trade unions should familiarise themselves with the various sectors of our economy in order that they may interpret their action and that of the Government correctly.

We have five sectors of economy, namely:-

1. *The State Sector.*
2. *The Large Scale Private Enterprise Sector.*
3. *The Joint State and Private Enterprise Sector.*
4. *The Co-operative Sector; and*
5. *The Small Scale Personal Private Sector reserved for Ghanaians.*

These five sectors are in the best interests of the national economy. And I hope the T.U.C. will study them and work out its policies and plan its organisations accordingly.

The cause of African redemption is noble and irresistible.

As long as we remain true to that cause—the cause of national freedom, independence and unity—we should have nothing to fear. We workers of Africa must therefore unite and unite with the progressive working people of the world. We have a continent to regain; freedom, respect and human dignity to attain.

That is why the Ghanaian trade unions, apart from their internal role of mobilising the workers for increased productivity, have also to wage a continental struggle to achieve African labour unity. The miners in Northern Rhodesia must know that they have something in common with the miners in our Ashanti Goldfields. The Dockers of Takoradi and Tema must have something in solidarity with the Dockers in Cape Town and Mombasa. We must find the means of exchanging delegations. Our miners must visit their mining friends in other parts of Africa; our construction friends on North, East and Central Africa. In everything we do must consolidate our unity and raise the whole struggle of African labour to a higher ideological level.

In the efforts of the Ghana T.U.C. to strengthen the all-Africa trade union federation in order to make it effective in our struggle against colonialism and oppression, you can always count on my support, and also the support of the Party and the Government

The African liberation struggle is gaining fresh victories every day, we should be on guard that neo-colonialism does not snatch from us, through the back-door, what we have won, through a hard and bitter fight. Their new tactics must be discovered and exposed to the African masses. Our cause today for African independence and unity can no longer be ignored by the world. It is a force to reckon with those who attempt to trifles with it hold themselves to ransom.

Your gathering here today is yet another demonstration of African solidarity. It is no longer possible to base the prosperity of some countries on the poverty of people in other parts of the world. That is why the whole struggle becomes a global one and I have no doubt that you will tackle your deliberations bearing in mind your responsibilities to your country and to mankind.

I would like to express my best wishes for the success of this convention. May your decisions be wise and profitable to our workers, people and our nation.

Mr. Chairman, I now have the pleasure to inaugurate this first biennial convention of the Trades Union Congress of Ghana.

10

THE OPENING OF ELECTRICITY AND WATER SUPPLIES FOR SUNYANI

Sunyani
March 27, 1962.

LADIES AND GENTLEMEN,

I recall with much pleasure my last visit to Sunyani in December, 1960, and the wonderful reception which was accorded to me and my party. I am glad to be with you again, and to share with you our joy in the completion of your new Water Works and Electricity Supplies Systems.

I wish to thank you all, chiefs and people of this Region for the enthusiastic reception I received when I arrived yesterday. I was much impressed by the obvious and spontaneous expression of loyalty and confidence in myself, the Party and the Government.

Since my arrival at your regional headquarters, I not the tremendous development which has taken place here since my last visit. The progress which has been made in the construction of the Sunyani airstrip is quite significant. I have also received encouraging reports about the many self-help projects which have been completed since my last visit.

Your Region has been able to achieve much during the three years of its existence. By making such a tremendous progress within so short a time, you, the chiefs and people of this region, have demonstrated your acceptance of the challenge presented to your regional autonomy, and I am happy to say that have justified the creation of this region.

I hope that the people of this Region will appreciate the advantages to be derived from these amenities and that they will readily pay their water-rate and electricity charges so as to help the maintenance of the machinery which will provide these amenities.

I congratulate the staff of the Water Supplies Division and the Electricity Division as well as all the other people who contributed to the construction of these projects.

Nananom, Ladies and Gentlemen, I shall now turn on the fountain and switch on the light. May the water that will flow here refresh and enliven all those who drink it, and may the light which will be transmitted from the Electricity Power House brighten your ways and be a source of inspiration to you all in the struggle for the social and economic reconstruction of Ghana.

11

APPEAL TO NATIONAL WORKERS
BROADCAST TO THE NATION

April 2, 1962

GOOD EVENING.

As from to-day our civil servants, public officers and workers in state enterprises throughout Ghana will have adopted the new hours of work recently decided upon by the Government. Our public officers are now called upon to work harder and a little longer than they did before. I know that many of you understand the reasons for the change, and will accept gladly this new arrangement.

As I said in Kumasi last week when I opened the first biennial conference of the Trade Union Congress, we must all, in our present stage of development, discard completely our old ideas about work. We have got to constantly remind ourselves that our total effort must be directed to providing honest and loyal service to the nation and as far as lies in our power, to the raising of production and productivity in our officers, our workshops, our garages, our classrooms and farms. By so doing, we make a positive contribution to the realisation of our socialist objectives which are for the ultimate good of all the people of Ghana.

The hours of work, which are to begin to-day, envisage that every worker will put in forty-four hours of work every week. But many representations have been made to me that the time of finishing, that is, 5 p.m., will prevent people from taking part in sporting and other social activities, and that this will, ultimately, affect the efficiency of the workers.

After careful consideration, I have decided that the number of working hours for public officers and workers in state enterprises should be fixed at forty-two hours instead of forty-four hours a week, and that office hours should be as follows: from Monday to Friday, 7.30 a.m. to 12.30 p.m. in the mornings and 2 p.m. to 4.30 p.m. in the afternoons, and on Saturday, 7.30 a.m. to 12 noon.

I hope that public officers and state workers will not only realise their obligations to the State, but also accept fully the responsibility which they share for the task of reconstruction in which we are engaged. The nation expects from you all maximum dedication to its service.

The party and the government are working and planning day and night to provide the people of Ghana with full employment, the widest possible opportunities for the development of the individual and the rising of their living standards. None of these can be achieved, however, without the establishment of national stability, internal security and national wealth and prosperity.

I would like to call upon the firms and shops to adapt themselves to these new hours of work and to finish a little later than they do at present, say, at 6 p.m. This should enable public officers and state workers to do their shopping in ample time after office hours without much inconvenience. I am sure in this way they will be making their contribution to the success of our national effort.

I would like now to refer to my speech in Kumasi on the 24th March about the pattern of business organisation in Ghana. I said then that foreign firms would have to re-invest in Ghana 60 per cent of their net profit after tax.

I would like to make quite clear what the objectives of this policy are. Firstly, it is to accelerate the growth of Ghana's capital stock. Secondly, it is to conserve foreign exchange and maintain the national reserves at a safe level. By doing these two things we hope to make Ghana economically strong and thereby to attract additional new foreign investment from all parts of the world.

We recognise of course that foreign companies have a duty to their shareholders and so while we ask our friends to share with us some of the sacrifices that we ourselves are making for the sake of Ghana's development I would like to emphasise that they will still be free to distribute to their shareholders 40 per cent of their net profit after income tax has been paid.

Moreover, where a company gives proof of having reinvested all or part of this 40 per cent in any one year (as may well be the case in new and expanding enterprises) appropriate allowance will be made in subsequent years.

And now countrymen: On Saturday, the Government asked all for the deportation of a number of persons, mostly Lebanese nationals, who have been found to be engaging in currency smuggling, illicit diamond dealing and the smuggling of our gold, currency notes and other negotiable securities out of the country. This activity constitutes a dangerous attack on the Ghana pound and therefore threatens our economy.

Our critics who do not, and care not to understand our policies and actions criticise us in a rather naive, uninformed and sometime even irresponsible manner. Some of them know the facts yet they criticise us for shear spite. Others do not know the facts and yet they constitute themselves in to our judges. We have a duty to ignore these criticisms, for we are determined to protect our nation and people from external and foreign subversions and intrigues, and from the evil manoeuvres of wreckers, extortionists and saboteurs.

We in Ghana have a record of which we are justly proud, of hospitality, racial tolerance and friendliness to all strangers within our midst. Foreign nationals in Ghana, however, whether they are visitors to our country or whether they are resident here, have equal responsibility not to indulge in any activities which are prohibited by our laws, or which are calculated to endanger the economy and security of the state.

We wish to work together to develop Ghana into a strong, prosperous and progressive nation. To those foreign nationals who are prepared to identify themselves with our cause, we shall give every co-operation, support and protection.

Let us all rise up to the challenge of our time, and, as never before, devote all our energies to the service of our country and the maintenance of its peace, stability and prosperity.

Goodnight.

12

WORK AND HAPPINESS

GHANA'S SEVEN-YEAR DEVELOPMENT PLAN

May 5, 1962

GOOD EVENING.

I have come to the microphone to talk to you about our country and its great Party—the Convention People's Party.

As you know, the Party has been in power since 1951. It has won many elections. On each occasion it issued a manifesto to the people specifying what it hoped to achieve and promising the things it would do. All of you can bear testimony to the fact that the Party has not only kept its word and its faith with the people, but also has to its credit a brilliant record of fulfilment.

The success of our Party in political action has been outstanding. Its basic approach to national and international problems has the fullest support of our people and of all true African patriots. In spite of the great storms that it has weathered, it has emerged through each one stronger and better equipped for the great struggle of liberation. All this action calls for first-class organisation; it can be truly and proudly said that our Party possesses one of the finest organisations of our time.

Organisation presupposes planning and planning demands a programme for its basis. The Government proposes to launch a Seven-year Development Plan in January, 1963. The Party therefore, has a pressing obligation to provide a programme upon which this plan could be formulated.

We must develop Ghana economically, socially, culturally, spiritually, educational, technologically and otherwise, and produce it as a finished product of a fully integrated life, both exemplary and inspiring.

This programme, which we call a programme for "Work and

Happiness" has been drawn up in regard to all our circumstances and conditions, our hopes and aspirations, our advantages and disadvantages and our opportunities or lack of them. Indeed, the programme is drawn up with an eye on reality and provides the building ground for our immediate scientific, technical and industrial progress.

We have embarked upon an intensive socialist reconstruction of our country. Ghana inherited a colonial economy and similar disabilities in most other directions. We cannot rest content until we have demolished this miserably structure and raised in its place an edifice of economic stability, thus creating for ourselves a veritable paradise of abundance and satisfaction. Despite the ideological bankruptcy and moral collapse of a civilisation in despair, we must go forward with our preparations for planned economic growth to supplant the poverty, ignorance, disease, illiteracy and degradation left in their wake by discredited colonialism and decaying imperialism.

In the programme which I am today introducing to the country through this broadcast, the Party has put forward many proposal. I want all of you to get copies if this programme, to read and discuss it and to send us any observation s or suggestions you may have about it.

Tomorrow, the National Executive Committee of the Party will meet to discuss the Party programme and officially present it to the nation. I feel sure that it will decide in favour of an immediate release of this programme to the people. The Party, however will take no action on the programme until the masses of the people have had the fullest opportunity of reviewing it. Remember that it is at the moment merely a draft programme and only your approval will finalise it.

At this present moment, all over Africa, dark clouds of neo-colonialism are fast gathering African States are becoming debtor-nations, and client States day in and day out, owing to their adoption of unreal attitudes to world problems, saying "no" when they should have said "yes", and "yes" when they should have said "no". They are seeking economic shelter under colonialist wings, instead of accepting the truth—that their survival lies in the political unification of Africa.

Countrymen, we must draw up a programme of action and later plan details of this programme for the benefit of the whole people. Such a programme is the one that the Party now brings to you, the people of Ghana, in the hope that you will approve it critically and help to make it a success.

We have a rich heritage. Our natural resources are abundant and varied. We have mineral and agricultural wealth and, above all, we have the will to find the means whereby these possessions can be put to the greatest use and advantage.

The Party's programme for work and happiness is a pointer to the way ahead, the way leading to a healthier, happier and more prosperous life for us all. When you have examined and accepted this programme, the Government and the people will base on it and initiate our Seven-Year Development Plan, which will guide our action to prosperity.

This programme constitutes for us a vigorous reminder that we must eschew complacency and push forward more determined than ever before to achieve our goal and, through work and enterprise, to create progress, prosperity and for our people.

The Eleventh Congress of the Party is scheduled to take place on the 10th of June. This Congress will give its final approval to the new Party programme.

Countrymen, we have carried out an important work of consolidation. We have stabilised the national structure and established solid security. We have done all this and more within the past ten years and we now prepare to move forward to the next stage.

We do so in the confident expectation that every one of us will do his duty and do it well. The national cause of socialist reconstruction demands sacrifice from us all. Each one of us must sacrifice a little for the total good of the whole people.

This programme for "Work and Happiness" is an expression of the evidence of the nation's creative ability, the certainty of the correctness of our Party line and action and the greatest single piece of testimony of our national confidence in the future.

Ghana is our country which we must all help to build. This programme gives us the opportunity to make our contribution towards the fulfilment of our national purposes.

As I look at the content of the programme and the matters it covers, such as Tax Reform, Animal Husbandry and Poultry Production, Forest Husbandry, Industrialisation, Handicrafts, Banking and Insurance, Foreign Enterprise, Culture and Leisure, I am convinced beyond all doubt that Ghana and Ghanaians will travel full steam ahead, conscious of their great responsibilities and fully aware that the materialisation of this bright picture of the future is entirely dependent on their active and energetic industry.

We cannot afford to fail. We cannot afford to think of failure. But if there is one thing we in this great Party have learnt, it is that nothing has been achieved or will ever be achieved without unstinted effort and the determination to succeed. Nothing succeeds like success. So all of us must tighten our belts and plunge head first into the fight for the urgent socialist reconstruction about which we have talked so much.

It is my sincere hope that each one of you will take an interest in this national exercise and make the Party programme for work and happiness a great success.

And now, Countrymen, I have been speaking to you about our Party programme. From this I turn to a subject of almost equal moment, because it affects what is to me of the greatest importance, namely, the maintenance of the Republic as by law established and the achievement of those aims which under our Constitution I have pledged myself as President to strive for.

An emergent country which attempts to follow a policy of socialism at home and a policy abroad of positive non-alignment, is challenging many vested interests. It would have been the most criminal folly for us not to take note of the lessons of contemporary history.

When you chose me as your President, I took an oath in which I swore that I would preserve and defend the Constitution and the I would do right to all manner of people according to law, without fear or favour, affection or ill will.

I should have been false to my oath had I allowed the Constitution to be overthrown by force, but I consider that the obligations which the Constitution imposes upon me not only call upon me to do justice, but also, wherever possible, to temper justice with mercy.

We have by no means passed through all our difficulties. The need for a Preventive Detention Act still remains, but I believe that the time has come when the security situation has improved sufficiently to allow a number of detainees to be released.

I have therefore ordered the immediate release of many of those at present under detention.

The Government had originally considered that anyone who had been previously detained and released, and who then again engages in subversive activities, should be liable to a maximum imprisonment of twenty years. On this matter, too, I consider that a gesture of reconciliation can be made. The maximum period of five years detention as provided in the existing law will be retained, but the Preventive Detention Act will be so amended as to provide that anyone released from detention who again indulges in subversion, shall be detained again up to the present maximum of five years, and may, in addition, lose all rights as a citizen.

There remains also the question of those few citizens who have fled abroad. In one or two cases detention orders have been made against subversive individuals who have since fled the country, and in the event of such people returning to Ghana, these orders would be reviewed. But in most cases, those who have fled from Ghana have done so because they had a bad conscience or else were frightened by some unscrupulous rumour-monger.

A general amnesty will be extended to all such persons. I call upon them to return and to put their energies into useful purposes for the good of the country. I give them the assurance that they will not be victimised in any way or subjected to any disability for any past act; so long as they remain loyal and law-abiding they will not only have nothing to fear, but will also be assured of the protection which the machinery of the law provides and to which everyone in this country is entitled.

Countrymen, now is the time for reconstruction. We have a gigantic task before us. In solving our problems even those who in the past believed that they could gain their ends by subversion can now, if only they give up illegal methods, find their way back into useful and fruitful work.

Goodnight.

13

REGRET AND FORGIVENESS

REPLY TO WELCOME ADDRESS BY CHIEFS AND PEOPLE OF SEKONDI/TAKORADI

May 26, 1962

NANANOM AND COMRADES,

I have listened carefully to your address of welcome and I thank you for all the things you have said.

The story of the last strike here is a sad one, and the less said about it the better. Some of you were misled and allowed yourselves to be used in a manner that struck at the very roots of States Security. However, all that is now past. We have all learnt a useful lesson—a lesson teaching us the importance of personal and national vigilance in guarding the security of our Party and our State.

It is important that we should remind ourselves constantly that Ghana is in a peculiar position. Because of our dynamic and uncompromising stand for Africa, we have incurred the inveterate hate of the imperialists and colonialists; because of our progressive outlook in regard to human dignity and equality, those who spurned the masses in the days of colonial rule and who thought they would rule the country when we attained independence, have become our detractors and traducers, wishing the Ghana Government were in the hands of puppets they could manipulate. We have a great responsibility, therefore, to guard our national security and to uphold the Constitution with the utmost jealousy and care.

The Convention People's Party is your Party. The Government is your own—the people's and the workers Government, and the measures we have introduced for improving the conditions of masses bear eloquent testimony to the keen interest which the Party and the Government take in the welfare and progress of the country.

We are moving forward at such a rapid pace, that none of you can afford to sit back unconcerned. If you do, you will be quickly overtaken by events.

We are proud, and you should be proud, too, that our struggle for freedom had some substantial beginnings here in Sekondi-Takoradi, and this should make you active guides for the Party and the Government. Never again should Sekondi-Takoradi go the way it went.

I accept your apology and take note of the firm vows and promises you make to-day. All I ask is that you should never again break faith with the Party. What has past should be a lesson for us to understand: that a people's revolution does not thrive on past achievements. It guards the present and pushes on to secure the future against counter-revolution and subversion.

I will cherish the memory of this act of repentance and reconciliation, and I am happy to inform you that I have directed that those of our workers who were dismissed and detained and whom the Government recently released, should be given back their jobs.

Nananom, Comrades and Friends: I thank you for the presents you have given me and I hope that to-day will mark the opening of a new and inspiring chapter in the relations between Sekondi/Takoradi and our great Party and Government.

14
STEP TO FREEDOM

NATIONALISTS' CONFERENCE OF AFRICAN FREEDOM FIGHTERS

June 4, 1962

FELLOW FREEDOM FIGHTERS, COMRADES AND FRIENDS,

It is my great pleasure to welcome you to Accra and to this conference of African Freedom Fighters and supporters of the growing movement for Africa's liberation and unity. It is good for our cause to have a periodic meeting of this kind, to examine our position in the great struggle to rid Africa completely and forget of imperialism and its hand-maidens, colonialism and neo-colonialism. It gives us the opportunity also to review our strength as well as that of the enemy, and to reorganise our forces and our strategy in order to carry struggle forward to victory.

We have shaped a destiny for ourselves, and no one can alter the course of that destiny. It is the destiny of complete freedom for Africa—the total liberation of our continent and its political and economic unification.

We have achieved some measure of success in this struggle for human freedom and dignity, nut we still have a great task ahead. We can only know the extent of our task and our own strength when we have examined and ascertained that of the enemy.

We are meeting here in Accra to perform precisely such a task, namely, to survey the forces at our disposal, to determined our position at this time, to assess correctly the enemy's forces and to plan our strategy and battle tactics for the final phase of the struggle for Africa's emancipation.

Who is the enemy?

The enemy is imperialism, which uses as its weapons colonialism and neo-colonialism. Let us be very clear about this. Let us also not lose sight of the real objective which is the liquidation of colonialism and imperialism in all its forms—political, economic and ideological—and the political unification of Africa.

Then we must ask:

What is imperialism and what are the forms it has taken and what other masks is it likely to put on?

Modern imperialism arose when capitalism had achieved both industrial and financial monopoly and the competition for raw materials and markets had made it imperative for the advanced industrialised countries to expand into the less advanced parts of the world. This phenomenon led to the partitioning of the world among the great powers. Asia and Africa were divided up among them.

Some of us think that because Asia has forced itself free of colonial control and much of Africa has done so too, the nature of imperialism has perhaps undergone a kind of changes. This thought is misleading, for the present devices of neo-colonialism and new imperialism has perhaps undergone a kind of change. This thought is misleading for the present devices of neo-colonialism and the new imperialist form that follows in the wake of African independence, give clear evidence of the continued active operation of imperialism in Africa.

At the end of the First World War, the victorious powers rearranged their spheres of influence in Africa. Re-division of boundaries was just as arbitrary as the original frontiers, and imperialism remained as impressive as ever, even though some of the masters had changed. The thing that has not changed was the extending arm of finance-capital, which was expanding its monopoly in ever-widening circles. Trading Corporations had begun to emerge and soon created themselves into giant monopoly combines. Great mining combines were linked up with banking capital in London, New York, Brussels, Paris, and Hamburg. All of them were intently milking Africa's resources, believing that the huge profits they were making would continue for a long time. How could they think otherwise, when it was possible to take up 99-year concessions on land and mines almost for nothing?

But one great thing had happened in Europe which was having, and was to continue to have, its repercussions upon subsequent history throughout the world. That was the October Revolution of 1917 in Russia, which spread rapidly throughout the Czarist empire and, overcoming the imperialist intervention, gave birth in 1922 to the Union of Soviet Socialist Republics Beginning with four republics, it has risen from a war-torn, undeveloped, largely agrarian land into a vast union of sixteen national republics, forming the second industrial state of the world.

The most far-reaching outcome of the consolidation of the Soviet Union was that it removed from the capitalist-imperialist orbit, one-sixth of the earth's surface. The withdrawal of the Soviet Union from the capital world retired what might well have become a very profitable sphere of investment for finance-capital.

There was a renewed fever for colonial expansion, which led to Mussolini's war on Ethiopia and West's backing off Japan's wars in Korea, Manchuria and China, the spoils of which they looked forward to sharing. A reconstructed Germany was also looking enviously at her former colonies in Africa.

Fellow Freedom Fighters and Friends: the colonial struggle develops unevenly. It has to press forward wherever it was strongest to create a break in the international imperialist chain. Thus the breaking of the imperialist chain at certain weak links has undermined the whole of the colonial system in Africa. The independent states that have emerged first have acted as a beacon light for the others, on whose behalf they have been charges with the responsibility of striking a blow. In this way, African nationalist thinking has been adjusting to internationalism within the continent, the developing process that must lead to the political unification of Africa.

But the objective of African unity can be seriously undermined by tribalism, which provides one of the happiest hunting grounds for the colonialist and neo-colonialist enemies of African independence and unity. The Congo is a typical example of how a country can be turned to the use of imperialist vested interests to subvert independence and lever off a most valuable part of the country for continued neo-colonialist exploitation.

In my view, unless we take this problem of tribalism very carefully in hand, it can undo all our valiant efforts to bring real independence to Africa. We all know the evils of colonialism, but there are some of us who do not appreciate the malevolent possibilities for infinite disruption, and even chaos, of uncontrolled tribalism, which can make havoc of our hopes and aspirations.

We know that the colonialists are past-masters in the policy of divide and rule. They are quick to seize on tribal differences which they discover among us and use these to pit one group against the other. Soon these superficial differences become exaggerated into serious political factions which sometimes lead to tragic fratricidal struggles within the same territory. You who are in the thick of the struggle in Angola, Mozambique, Portuguese Guinea and elsewhere know this game too well. You must guard against it; guard against it by forging a common united front against the enemy. The dangers it opens up and the manipulations to which it can be put are too numerous and too threatening for us to ignore its urgent demand for critical and constructive attention. Failure in this task would only risk all the effort and sacrifices that we have made so far in our common cause and place in utter jeopardy the future peace and development of this continent. I therefore charge you to place it high on your agenda and give it your most thoughtful and creative consideration.

Colonial rule has left a high degree of illiteracy among our people, and we all know that in conditions of ignorance and superstition, it is easy enough to fan internecine feuds. This menace can be met by unity among the leaders and the creation of a nation-wide, firmly knit political organisation, receiving the most complete loyalty and devoted service from all its members, especially its officers and organising officials in the field. But it is imperative for he problem to be seized and dealt with, and for everyone of us to be on our guard against its creeping insinuations and menacing possibilities.

Colonial rule has also left the masses of our people poverty-stricken and disease-ridden, while enormous quantities of mineral and agricultural wealth were drained out of Africa year in and year out. From the labours of our people, vast profits have been wrung for industrial and financial monopolies. In the Portuguese colonies, in the Belgian Congo, in the Union of South Africa, in the Rhodesias, Nyasaland, Kenya and other settler areas forced labour and slave conditions are the lot of millions Africans, whose lands have been expropriated and imposing hut and poll taxes and bending the customary traditions of communal service to the needs of settler farmers, mining companies, and land concessionaires. Legislation has turned many millions of Africans into helots in their own land. It will take all the tricks of expurgation and the greatest manipulation of truth ever fashioned to wipe out of the pages of history the dreadful things and monstrous wrong that have been inflicted on our people by those who came here, so they said, to bring their civilising mission to this vast and great continent. There is not one of us who has not, in a minor or major degree, felt the oppressive heel of colonial rule. I am not making this point merely in order to harrow you with ugly memories. Many of you have been confronted only too recently with the shocking actualities of calculated oppression to be able at this moment to push them out of mind. I raise the point so that it will stay in your minds when you may be tempted by the seductive promises of neo-colonialism to forget the real character of colonialism, and be persuaded away from your own true interests and those of Africa.

For to-day we must each see ourselves as part of Africa in order that we may face colonialist-imperialism and its new form, neo-colonialism, on a continent-wide front. When the first All African People's Conference met here in Accra in December of 1958, I pointed out that: "Our deliberations must be conducted in accord and our resolution must flow out of unity. For unity must be the keynote of our actions. Our enemies are many and they stand ready to pounce upon and exploit our every weakness. They tell us that this particular person or that particular country has greater or more favourable potentialities than the other. They do not tell us that we should unite, that we are all as good as we are able to make ourselves once we are free. Remember always that you have four stages to make:-

(1) the attainment of freedom and independence;
(2) the consolidation of that freedom and independence;
(3) the creation of unity and community between the free African states;
(4) the economic and social reconstruction of Africa."

What has happened since in on way invalidates these assumptions. In the face of recent and present events, they have, in fact, a greater urgency than ever. When the first conference of independent African states assembled in Accra in April 1958, there were eight independent African states. To-day, we have increased our number to nearly thirty, with more on the way; but the problems which plagued us then still remain: how to maintain the hard-won independence of those of us who are free and, at the same time, assist the burning struggle of our brothers still fighting for their independence on this continent. The answer, too, is the same. We must unify ourselves in policy and in action, both between all of us who are independent, and between the independent states and the still unliberated millions on this continent.

We have, it true, recorded in the pages of contemporary history, signal success in the continuing struggle for human freedom and dignity. But there still remains the gigantic task ahead of redeeming from the grinding heel of colonialist-imperialism the parts of Africa still under its yoke. Africa is for Africans and unless those within our gates can accept the rule of the majority, they must either pick themselves up and go or be forced to surrender to our just demands.

We do not, for instance, accept the South African argument that the land it occupies was no man's land when the first settlers came and met it unoccupied. This is Africa and the land they settled upon is African land belonging to Africans whether they were there or not upon the settlers' arrival. Africa is not an extension of Europe and if Europeans want to develop a separate nation, then they must find a place on their own continent to do so. They cannot expect to remain here, to live upon and lord it over an African majority in a master-slave relationship that derives our fellow Africans in the South of every human right and dignity.

Nor do we countenance the Central African Federation, forced upon seven million Africans for the benefit of three hundred thousand Europeans, determined to extend the arrogant assumptions of racial superiority over ever wider stretches of our continent. We have no time for the platitudes about aim at continuing a jack-boot system which will keep the Africans at the hewer-of-wood and drawer-of-water level.

We are equally opposed to the sham constitutions that are being foisted on Swaziland and Bechuanaland, the British protectorate enclaves in South Africa, which are nothing but a sop to the popular demand for democratic government in preparation for independence. The traditional elements are being favoured as administrative instruments for the obstruction of progress to full independence. In Basutoland, the third British protectorate in South Africa, the intent is apparent in the neglect to transfer any kind of power to the people. It is easy to understand that the South African Union could not tolerate three completely independent African States within the very borders of what she claims to be her territory.

The hurricane of change that is raging through Africa and razing to the ground many of the bastions of colonialism, is a warning that we Africans mean to be masters on our own continent. But we should be doing ourselves a great disservice if we were to sink into smug complacency and take it for granted that time is all on our side and that, because history is with us, the total independence of Africa will fall into our hands like a ripe mango. This is decidedly not the case. The forces arrayed against us are—and I use the word most carefully—formidable. They are entrenched and powerful. They are, as I have taken some pains to explain, the forces of imperialism acting through their instruments, colonialism and neo-colonialism, ably assisted by the agents of the cold-war. They operate in world-wide combinations at all levels: political, economic, military, cultural, educational, social and trade; and through intelligence cultural and information services. They operate from European and African centres, using agents who I am ashamed to say, are often unpatriotic sons of Africa, buying personal satisfactions with the betrayal of their countries' safety and integrity. They seduce leaders of the African political , trade union and people's organisations, thus creating rifts and quarrels within the national fronts.

On the broader fronts, they are massing their forces in a determined effort to stay the advance of African liberation and the march to unity. It is not accidental that the countries of the European Common Market are those spearheading the North Atlantic Treaty Organisation, the imperialist powers who have brought in the vassals, Spain and Portugal. Portugal has, in fact, since the wars of the Spanish succession, 1700-1714 been a protectorate of Britain, which has enjoyed special trading and concessionary rights in both Portugal and Portuguese territories for over two hundred years. It is not difficult to understand, therefore, why Britain has not raised her voice against the atrocities in Angola and the other Portuguese territories, and actually supported Portugal's preposterous claim that Goa, in India, was an integral part of the metropolitan country.

The arms and troops that are pouring into Angola cannot be regarded in isolation from the international organisations of imperialism and the cold war militarism with which they are most definitely linked. It is absurd to think that Portugal, one of the poorest countries in Europe, could support so large an army so well equipped as that which is defending her colonial possessions in Africa without the active aid she must be receiving from the North Atlantic Treaty Organisation.

Nor can we look upon the way in which South Africa is busily building up an armed force equal to any held by the nations of Europe without scenting the international implications that are obviously involved. She has, we hear, a secret military pact with Portugal. And the interlocking imperialist interests collected in Congo and the Rhodesians, Angola and Mozambique, which are also linked with the great mining and financial combines operating in South Africa, create a chain of allies which seriously threatens both the fight for extending African emancipation from colonialism and the independence of the new states.

Now that African independence has been achieved over a large part of the continent and the national consciousness of Africans from north to south, from east to west, is adding momentum to the struggle for independence, every kind of means is being used by the colonialists to arrest its progress and defeat its objective. They are attempting many methods, some sinister, some beguiling, to wreck our efforts. They strike antipathetic postures. On one side, they perform acts calculated to strike fear; on the other, they try to hoodwink us with fictitious gifts which superficially pander to our hopes and aspirations. They are the frenzied attempts to deflect our purpose, to weaken our determination.

Of late, atrocities of the worst possible kind have been perpetrated against Africans. The horror of Portuguese atrocities appals all right-minded people. The massacres at Dembos, Golungo Alto, Ambaca, Dondo, Cacuso, Libolo and others, will be to the eternal shame of the present Portuguese regime. Troops drafted into Baixe de Cassange to shoot down Africans demonstrating against abusive practices, killed over eight thousand innocent people. Planes bombed unarmed, defenceless men and women. The Portuguese record in Angola, in Mozambique, Guinea, Sao Tome and Principle is a long, repetitive story of murder, robbery and active persecution of Africans. The intensity of the new repression is illustrated by the recent flight of more than eighty thousand persons into the Congo.

On the other hand, it is interesting to note the latest solicitude of those responsible for the Sharpville massacre for the "national rights" of a South African tribe singled out for the favour of racial independence, as the settler rulers of the Union are pleased to call it. This is segregated government by chiefs of the Pondoland tribe within its circumscribed reserve makes a pitiful mockery not only of the meaning of freedom but of the dignity of the Africans compelled to accept this travesty of independence. It is difficult to believe that world opinion will be hoodwinked by what is nothing more than a thinly disguised trick to prove that South Africa is not against African freedom within segregation; but that she is only against African independence that will assure the democratic right of the indigenous majority to rule an alien minority. In any event, it is an extraordinary division of independence which could only have been devised by a people too blind to see its impossibility against the activities of mid-twentieth century developments, both political, industrial, economic and social. The theory that a minority of settlers can continue to subjugate, to dominate, rob and enslave millions of Africans has no reality in our present world of expanding nationalism and more and more technical means of production. And the idea that the Union can continue to exist within its own frontiers for any length of time on the output of extractive industries, plantation farming, and a ramshackle industrial machine, run by near-slave labour, is very much open to question.

I must again urge the United Nations to see to it that its own declaration on the liquidation of colonialism is given practical effect without further delay. So long as colonialism exists in Africa, Africans cannot help talking the way we do now, and mankind cannot escape the constant threat of war. Africa therefore appeals to the United Nations to live up to its reputation as the greatest bastion of world peace, and demands that a meeting of this year's United Nations session should be devoted to the problem of colonialism in Africa. Furthermore, the United Nations should make a firm declaration calling upon the Colonial Powers to quit Africa by the 31st December, 1962. The Freedom Fighters assembled in this historic conference must also call upon all the Colonial Powers to withdraw from Africa by the same date. It is in their interest and in the interest of world Peace that this should be so.

It is folly for the colonialists to think that they can hold back forever the progress of history. The process of change is inherent in the interplay of social, economic and political forces. It is true that these can be hindered and impeded, and even bent to different purposes; but not forever. How, we who are concerned with the immediacy of African independence and unity, are not prepared to wait upon the evolution of history. We are determined to give history a revolutionary push, or if I may boast a little, to push rather harder the revolutionary wheel that we freedom fighters have already turned a considerable way across Africa.

The instruments of slaughter, the harshness of the repressions, the intensification of the oppression being brought against Africans as independence advances over our continent, all these devices place a heavy obligation upon us who are independent to move our forces forward and make it plain to the colonialists and imperialists that we are adamant in out purpose to destroy colonialism in Africa. No lukewarm approach will avail. We must bring all our battalions into array to match the skill of our enemy. We must adopt a positive all-out anti-colonialist, anti-imperialist attack, and this quickly, for we cannot afford the luxury of delay. Time acts for the enemy no less than for ourselves.

Let us, therefore, examine our position seriously and objective, to see how well we have managed so far, and evaluate our points of weakness and the necessary remedies. Let us determine what modifications are needed to adjust our strategy to counter the movements of the enemy and overcome him.

This requires some plain speaking, and for the sake of Africa, let us speak plainly.

As I see it, our greatest danger stems from disunity and the inability to see that the realisation of our hopes and aspirations, the realisation of our objective of total African independence, and of our future progress and prosperity, is inextricably bound up with the necessity to unity our policy and actions in connection with the continuing struggle for independence and the greater task of economic and social reconstruction beyond it.

We need unity within the ranks of the independence states, unity within the ranks of the freedom fighters still struggling to achieve independence; and unity between the already independence states and the freedom fighters.

I do not think that too much stress can ever be laid upon this need for unity. It is our unity that the imperialist agencies are trying by every means to obstruct and sever. It is the idea of African Unity that they fear most. It seems only intelligent, therefore, for us to close our ranks and compact our forces.

If we independent states were unified in a political and economic union, having a common foreign and defence policy, controlling a unified military command, we should be in a much stronger position to assist the territories still struggling for independence. An over-all economic plain, covering united on a continental basis, must increase our total industrial and economic power; hence, our combined strength, reinforced by a common purpose would add enormously to the united front which we could turn against the enemy. So long as we remain disunited, so long as we remain balkanised, whether regionally or in separate national units, we shall be at the mercy of imperialism and neo-colonialism.

We must therefore face the issue of African Unity now; for only unity will make the artificial boundaries and regional demarcations imposed by colonialism obsolete and superfluous. African Unity will thus provide an effective remedy for border disputes internecine troubles. In a united Africa there would be no frontier claims between Ethiopia and Somalia or between Zanzibar and Kenya, Guinea and Liberia or between Togoland and the Ivory Coast.

because we would regard ourselves as one great continental family of Nations.

Among the new states in Africa are some which, through fragmentation, have been left so weak economically, that they are unable to stand on their own feet. This is the result of a deliberate policy of the withdrawing colonial powers, who have created in Africa several small, feeble and unstable and unviable states, in the hope of ensuring their continued dependence upon the former colonial power for economic and technical aid. Indeed, the intention goes farther than that, and is more insidious. It is to produce a political atmosphere as dangerous to the safety and progress of African independence as that which followed the establishment of the many friable nations which were created in Eastern Europe by the Congress of Vienna (1814-1815). The underlying design is to induce national jealousies and rivalries such as nourished the outbreak of the First World War. At best, it is hoped that such a policy may lead open conflict. At worst, it must present tough obstacles to the movement for total African freedom and African unity. This is the inner plan of neo-colonialism, the instrument of imperialism. While relinquishing political rule it contrives to control the foreign and internal policy if the states it still dominates through the bestowal of material aid.

In effect, only the outward forms have changed, but the substance of colonialism remains. Foreign imports are still protected, local development is clamped down, social progress is retarded, and fiscal policy is controlled from the metropolitan capital. The impact of these semi-independent states on the liberation of Africa is calamitous. Bound up as they are with the policies of their sponsors, they are unable to take a determined, independent line on issues involving the colonialists and the still enslaved peoples on this continent. Some of the leaders, it must be confessed, do not see the struggle of their brother Africans as part of their own struggle. Even if they did, they would not be free to express their solidarity. Thus rifts are consciously created by the imperialists between Africans, which they can sit back and watch with sly satisfaction, as well as contempt for those who fail to see how they are being used against Africa's best interests. Regrettably, those states include some who were among the freedom fighters of yesterday and who, having won their independence, are willing to drop it for some token aid, and thereby deny to those still struggling for freedom even their moral supports. Here is a phenomenon against which all African freedom fighters must be on their guard and resist to the utmost.

Even though I appreciate the difficulties facing us, I must admit I find it strange to watch some of us returning willingly to the colonialist fold. This time they don't even have the excuse of being forced to subject themselves to foreign domination. It makes one wonder why so much effort and sacrifice, and so many lives, were given up to the achievement of independence in the first place, if it can be so quickly and easily surrendered. Unhappily for us, colonialism creates in some, intellectual allegiances which are not serve at the moment of independence, but remain to condition loyalties away from Africa towards the metropolis which draws them. They are unable, it would appear, to accept the idea that Africans can get together to make a viable and going concern of a combined African continent, but rather see their salvation in coming together in associations like the Franco-African Community mooted recently at Bangui.

Although there are many here who speak English, French, Spanish or Portuguese, nevertheless we are all African—Africans fighting for Africa's independence, Africa's unity, Africa's future.

I have said that I understand the difficulties of these states which are drawing away from the African community back into that Europe. Faced with the demands of their people for rising standards of living and better social conditions, but charged with economic that can hardly meet the recurrent expenses of administration and maintenance, they are in a dilemma. And standing at their elbows are the neo-colonialist agents, beckoning them back with a smile into the web of imperialism, though it may have a new look this time and offer the irresistible bait of immediate help will be far outweighed, as they will experience with no great loss of time, by the knots into which their economies will be tied by the Euro-African association. Imperialism does not change its nature; it only changes its front. It still needs colonial appendages, whether in name or in fact, to exploit and, at the same time, to support its cold war strategy.

In the face of the serious threat to our economy and independence in Africa, we must begin to build immediately our own continental Common Market, for it is easy for anyone who studies the Common Market Organisation closely to realise that the Common Market is aimed at harnessing the African countries to satisfy the profit-lust of the imperialist bloc and to prevent us from following an independent neutralist policy. It is also easy to see that the imperialist and colonialists are determined to retain the African countries in the position of suppliers of cheap raw material.

If we do not resist this threat, and if we throw in our lot with the Common Market, we shall doom the economy of Africa to a state of perpetual subjection to the economy of western Europe. This will of course hinder the industrialisation of our young African states. It is impossible to think of economic development and national independence without possessing an unfettered capacity for maintaining a strong industrial power. The activities of the Common Market are therefore fraught with dangerous political and economic consequences for the Independent African States. The organisation constitutes an attempt to replace the old system of colonial exploitation by a new system of collective colonialism which will be stronger and more dangerous than the old evils we are striving to liquidate from our continent.

There is an alternative to the Euro-African association, with its deadly implications for Africa's independence and progress. It is an African Economic Community, in which we can all pool our production and our trade, to the common advantage. It is not difficult to imagine that the neo-colonialists will describe this as a pooling of poverty. It is, however, too simple a distortion of fact. Africa is rich and not poor, as the great wealth that has been taken out of our continent over five centuries of despoliation and extortion very well proves. Africa has immense actual and potential wealth. Gold, diamonds, copper, manganese, bauxite, iron, ore, uranium, asbestos, chrome, cobalt , a host of other minerals, our essential agricultural produce, have all been drained away by colonialist-imperialism. Africa is far from being poor. It is Africans who are poor, because of the uncounted profit that has been made out of the exploitation of their labour and their lands. If we are being baited to enter a European Community we must have something that community needs—and needs badly, when it pretends to offer a bonus by way of aid. When Greeks come bearing gifts, should we not look them well in the mouth, if I may mix my metaphor? But I am sure you get my meaning. When we new, untried inexperienced states are flattered into European alliances, we enter not as equals, but as suppliers of primary products at the generosity of industrial converters. How generous they can be, we have learned from our sad experience over a good long time. Who fixes prices? Who can play off one against the other by allowing the goods of associates in free of tariff and placing a tariff on others? As long as it is possible to deal with is singly, we are at the mercy of the imperialists rather than their generosity. And we shall find ourselves in the same old cleft stick of receiving the lowest possible prices for our raw materials, while those of us who are obliged to buy their manufactured goods, because of being members of their associations, will pay for them through the nose. These same states will find themselves tied up in knots which will prevent their going into an open market for their needs of goods and capital investment. And, above all, they will lose their option of non-alignment and find themselves dragged into the diplomacy of imperialist cold war politics which will operate against the independence and intrinsic interest of Africa. Those of us who cannot through these implications can only be suffering from an intense myopia.

Within our African Community, our pooled production will place us in a position to bargain for higher prices, and so secure greater revenues, out of which we can invest in our development. At the same time, we can trade freely among ourselves and buy from overseas in the cheapest markets. We can turn for aid to those sources which will give us the most suitable terms while leaving us free to follow our own internal and external policy. But more even than this narrow co-operation, we need the wider continental economic plan, which will allow us, within unity, to exploit Africa's tremendous resources for our common welfare and greater African development and progress.

If we are really sincere in our desire to see the end of imperialism in Africa unity, we should turn away from any from of association with Europe which, through its neo-colonialist control of our policies, will help rather to sustain that imperialism than undermine it. It is bad enough that our economies, as a legacy of colonial rule, are imperialist-controlled, and that we have to strive by every means to rid ourselves of this economic imperialism and secure our development and progress on solid African foundations. This is another reason why we should come together in a unified African economic plan, which, operating on a continental scale, can make a solid attack on imperialist domination in Africa.

We should, without delay, aim at the creation of a joint African military command. There is little wisdom in our present separate efforts to build up and maintain defence forces which, in any case, would be ineffective in any major conflict. If we examine this problem realistically, we would ask, which single African state could protect itself against an imperialist aggressor? And how much more difficult this will be when some states are allowing the imperialists to maintain bases on their territories? I have already referred to the military force which South Africa is raising and the danger it poses for the new African states and the struggle of those still in chains. Only our unity can provide us with anything like adequate protection. If we do not unite and combine our military forces, South Africa, along with her allies, or any other colonialist-imperialist power, can pick us off one by one. Not only that; some of us, out of a sense of insecurity, may be drawn into making defence pacts with the imperialists which will endanger the security of all us.

It follows that if we set up in Africa a common economic planning organisation and a joint military command, we shall have to work out and adopt a common foreign policy to give political direction to our continental development and our continental defence.

Fellow Freedom Fighters, you may perhaps wonder why I have dwelt at some length with these problems of the unity of independent African States and what relevance they have to your immediate problems of how to overcome the obstacles standing in the way of your own struggle for independence. I think I have answered any such questions by pointing out the dangers to the whole subject of your fight for freedom in the fragmentary state of Africa at this present time. Moreover, the moment you have achieved your independence, you will be faced with the practical problems of protecting that independence and securing your viability in order to lay the foundations on which to build up economic and social development. You must know where you are going, what avenues of support await you, which will contribute to your real consolidation and protection and meet the problems that will confront you.

These problems can best be met within a unified Africa, and it should be possible, in the higher reaches of our endeavour, to devise a constitutional structure which will secure the objectives I have outlined and yet preserve the sovereignty of each of the countries joining the union. Countries within the union will naturally maintain their own constitutions and continue to use their national emblems and national anthems and other symbols and paraphernalia of sovereignty.

Regional association and territorial groupings can only be other forms of balkanisation unless they are conceived within the framework of a continental union. There are existing models which we can modify or adapt into our pattern. The United States of America, the Soviet Union, India and China have proved the efficacy of unions embracing large stretches of land and population. When the first thirteen states of America tried to promote the idea of a United States, this was ridiculed as an empty dream and vigorously resisted by many. To-day, America is the foremost industrial country in the world, and the states within her union now number fifty. And who would have thought that almost a hundred different peoples at various levels of economic, social and political development could have been welded into the mighty state which the Soviet Union has become in such a short space of time?

The example of Europe, which is left in confusion after centuries of mutually destructive economic warfare and competition, because it failed to build a sound foundation for common political action and understanding, should be a lesson for us all. But with the exigencies created by the shrinking of empires, the growing socialist world and the needs generated by the greater productive capacities inherent in present-day techniques, even Europe is now beginning to seek its common associations. It is paradoxical, therefore, that some African states should be turning away from their proper African affiliations to those of another continent. Rather we should all be working ceaselessly to bring to fruition the fond hope of African unity to which we all give lip service and to which most of us are resolutely dedicated.

Let me here say a few words about the development in what looked like a hopeful move towards the unity of the Caribbean islands. We regard West Indians as our brothers, for they have strong ties of kinship with us here in Africa. They, like us, have suffered and are still suffering the iniquities of colonial oppression. I think it is only right that we should show concern over any development which tends to under mine their solidarity and progress, and have indeed been saddened by the failure of the attempt at federation. How can these little island hope to stand by themselves in the future any better than they have done in the past?

When the trend is towards the creation of bigger units of economic viability, it is most distressing to find that some of our brothers across the Atlantic seem to be unaware of the vital need of widest possible federation, drawn together by a central government with sufficient powers to make the principle of unified progress a working possibility. It would be tragic, not only for West Indians, but also for Africans and other people of African descent, if the islands of the West Indies were to remain apart. For we have reposed so much hope and faith in the emergence of the Caribbean isles as united states, free and progressive, federated in strength and purpose, and contributing substantially to the total success of all our peoples. I hope that West Indian leaders, who are men of learning and progress, will see the folly and danger of this disuniting development and arrest the process for the good of all concerned.

Here in Africa, the increasing activity of freedom fighters all over the continent is one of the most hopeful signs of the victory that must crown our efforts. Many have lost their lives. Many—far too many—have been mown down. Let their sacrifices spur us on to ever greater effort, to add to the great achievements that have already marked our struggle.

Let us now stand in silence for one minute in homage to those who have fallen in battle for Africa's freedom.

After seven long years, the French Government has made a

standstill agreement with our Algerian brothers, and we pay our tribute to the heroes of the Algerian Liberation Front. Many thousands have died in order that a true and progressive Algeria might live. The great self-restraint which the people of Algeria have shown in face of extreme provocation by the European Secret Army Organisation—the O.A.S.—is evidence of their national maturity and balanced political judgment. The obvious objective of these attacks is to nullify the Evian Agreement by inciting the Algerian people to hit back *en masse* and create sympathy for the O.A.S. cause. It is reassuring that the Algerian people, by and large, have remained clam in the face of extreme and wanton provocation, thus defeating the main purpose of the vengeful attacks of the O.A.S.

It is, however, becoming increasingly questionable whether the truce, in face of the obvious inability or, perhaps we might call it refusal, of the French to deal effectively with the subversive actions of the counter-revolutionary organisation in Algeria, can continue. To the Algerian Provisional Government we extend our esteem of the high sense of leadership they have exhibited before the temptations of retaliatory action, and assure them once again that all true and genuine sons of Africa stand resolutely by them in any course of action they may take to ensure the final victory of an utterly independent Algeria.

The gains that the freedom fight in African has made in a few years are astounding. No one would ever have believed that country after country could so rapidly have gained their independence. Not long ago—not yet ten years away—certain African leaders were still shy even of using the word "independence". They talked about "decolonisation", about "self-government", about "self-determination", etcetera. In fact, it was only at the Cotonou conference of the P.R.A. in August, 1958, that the word "independence" came out into the open in French West and Equatorial Africa. And even then, certain leaders tried to soft-pedal it as though it were indecent to give it forthright expression.

Popular pressure in the African lands is determining the question of independence, as it will determine African unity.

Unfortunately some of our leaders are eagerly attempting to demonstrate their affinity with the European cultures and philosophies, from which they can cut off only with harmful results to our African destiny.

Africa's interests are in Africa. That is why bellow the leadership throughout the independent states and within the freedom struggle that is going on in the unliberated parts of the continent, there is a surge towards unity which, if properly guided, can bring about the desired objective. The slogan of African unity is to-day on every lip. But there are those who have it only on their lip as a means of concealing their links with foreign interests and to hoodwink the millions of African workers and peasants who look eagerly forward to an upward change in their poverty-striken lives.

It is doubtful whether this facade can long deceive the people, for it breaks faith with them. And after all, if the principle is maintained that sovereignty is rooted in the people, they must use this sovereignty to secure governments wedded to Africa's true interests in genuine independence. Freedom Fighters of African must therefore closely watch the unfolding scene of African independence and development and make sure that no government shall deceive the rightful aspirations of the people and remain in power. Imperialist plans must be frustrated by making it impossible for neo-colonialism to recruit agents and retain them in the seats of power. This is no small task, but it a task which we must tackle in the supreme interest of Africa. It is part and parcel of the greater task of achieving Africa's total independence and unification, the plan for the winning of which we are here to determine.

In the prosecution of this task, we must endeavour to eliminate all those trends that will hamper our victory, and number and enlist all those forces that can support and join our struggle for colonialism's final overthrow in Africa. Some of these I have already dealt with; others I shall be coming to. First of all, we must recognise and acknowledge that our struggle is in Africa and that the brunt must fall upon us Africans. After all, it is *our* struggle. It is a struggle against the strongest combination of forces the world has ever seen: twentieth century imperialism in the epoch of the cold war. Despite their outward expressions of sympathy and understanding, we must discount any likelihood of real help in our struggle from the interested powers. They are, as we know busily carrying on their neo-colonialist intrigues behind their hypocritical protestations. Against this, we can counter the expansion of the non-aligned states, whose pressure at the United Nations has secure a certain response to the demand for an examination of the slave conditions in the Portuguese and South-west African territories, and in Ruanda Urundi and the Central African Federation.

While we cannot rely entirely upon United Nations action as a determining factor in the struggle, yet as we intensify our activities, the organisation can be utilised as an increasingly effective deterrent in connection with the more outrageous forms of colonial oppression. Whether we shall ever be able to secure its intervention actively on the side of the struggle in the event of open attack from the heavily armed colonial powers, will depend very much upon the unity of policy and action between the African states, and the support they can mobilise in the Security Council.

Though, as I say, we do not look for help among the imperialist governments in the struggle for independence and unity, yet there are many people within their countries whose sympathy and moral support we know we have. I know that Freedom Fighters have also received their active and material help in a number of ways. But as these friends cannot influence their governments, there is no possibility of our depending upon them to move their support to the battleground of Africa. However, we must not overlook the struggle which some sections of the European working class and intelligentsia are bringing out into the open against colonial governments in Africa. Here there is a definite link between our struggle and the working class battling for democratic rights and liberties against the metropolitan colonial governments. Both struggles are aimed at the same target: the destruction of colonialism and repressive administration. The simultaneous assault in the colonies and the metropolis helps to weaken the colonial power through the division of the forces it must deploy at both ends. It is possible that our struggles could be joined, on the absolutely clear and accepted understanding that we shall brook no interference with our right to independence.

Our other forces are within Africa, and they are within the independent states and the remaining colonial territories. They reside in the peoples and their organisations. They are in the trade unions, the farmers and peasants associations, the cooperatives, the youth movements, the women's organisations, the political parties, in fact, in every unit of nationalist endeavour.

The farmers of Africa have initiated their continental union, which joins not only members from the independent countries but also from the still dependent territories. We cannot keep fighting on empty stomachs, and our farmers have a great duty to keep us reasonably fed for the struggle. Their wisdom in coming together to form a union of African farmers gives hope sand confidence to all of us that a significant step has been taken in Africa unity.

The African trade unions have a particularly pressing responsibility to discard antiquated ideas about the separation of trade union activities from politics and to constitute themselves into an active vanguard in our political operations. Credit, therefore, must go to those who have joined the All African Trades Union Federation—the A.A.T.U.F. It is time for Africa to have her own independent, continental trade union apex body, which will owe allegiance to Africa's struggle for independence and economic and social reconstruction. The international Confederation of Free Trade Unions (the I.C.F.T.U.) represents the ideology of the capitalist countries. The World Federation of Trade Unions (the W.F.T.U.) represents the ideology of the socialist countries. We in Africa, who are committed to a policy of non-alignment, can only steer clear of extra-African entanglements by raising our own continental trade union organisation with its own ideology and freedom from external pressures. The I.C.F.T.U. has been at considerable pains and gone to considerable expense to infiltrate the African trade union movement and to seduce African trade union leaders away from an African stand and viewpoint. Within the context of the anticolonial struggle, the very organisation of a trade union is a political act, as those who remember the history of the Chartist movement in England will understand. And in the tasks of reconstruction after the attainment of independence, they have a special role to play in rallying the working class around a programme aimed at raising the standard of life of the mass of people. Where the government is a popular government, the African trade union movement is identified with the government programme, and thereby becomes its ally in securing its implementation. The trade union movement in Africa has already proved itself in the independence struggle, and our All African Trade Union Federation can be of inestimable aid in pushing these last stages to final victory. Its job is to cement the bonds of solidarity and union between the workers in all the territories and give its active support against the brutal exploitation of our comrades in the dependent territories.

One of the remarkable phenomena of our times is the way in which the colonial youth and women have accepted the challenge of the independence struggle and play their active part in it. All the way through the Algerian war, during our own militant activities here in Ghana, and as far as I can judge, in all the territories where the fight has erupted into open battle, whether short or prolong, our young people and women have aided their fathers and brothers, their husbands and sons in all manner of ways. They have acted as messengers, as sentries, as watchdogs, as providers and purveys of food and succour. They have even acted as spurs to push their hesitant menfolk into the thick of the struggle.

To-day, our youth organisations are interpreting their enthusiasm and aspirations into activities which support the fight for freedom and unity in Africa. Always the most oppressed, the slavery and misery of colonial oppression stung our African women into action, and they still remain in the front line if the battle in ever-increasing numbers. Here in Ghana, women played a most important part in the attainment of independence. They are now seriously engaged in our national reconstruction, and are dedicated to the cause of African unity. African womanhood in general is dedicated to the cause of liberation from colonialism, and Freedom Fighters should do everything to encourage our women to bring their effective efforts to the cause.

Fellow Freedom Fighters, we have told the world in clear terms, at every conceivable opportunity, that Africa has a vested interest in peace. We sincerely believe that others also cherish a similar interest in peace and that generally the world abhors violence. We must make it crystal clear, however, that we do not subscribe to the principle of peace at any price. It is true that we are prepare to pay an unbelievably high price for peace. We recognise the dangers of war implicit in the chain of events on this continent which has brought a high degree of armament to West, Central and South Africa, and which are linked with our struggle for independence and unity. Yet we are not prepared to retreat from the struggle one inch. On the contrary, we are firmer than ever in our determination to carry it forward to a triumphant conclusion, whatever the cost. For we are resolved that this continent shall not continue half-free, half-slave, not only because the independence of our states is threatened so long as a single colonial territory remains, but because we must help to win for our brothers their inalienable right to determine their own destiny. Moreover, the liquidation of imperialist-colonialism in Africa is in itself a profound act of peace, while the unity of this continent will constitute a great bulwark for the positive stabilisation of world amity and concord. For it will eliminate those causes of conflict tied up in the scramble for spheres of influence, and controlled sources of raw materials and markets.

We can endure the exasperation of protracted constitutional devices, calculated to delay independence and sovereignty. We can even submit to the process of the piecemeal granting of freedom to us, accepting the ridiculous judgment of those who have set themselves up as umpires of our progress, and who invariably proclaim our unripeness for self-government. But we shall not tolerate the application of violence against us simply because we demand our freedom. There are several effective ways in which we shall resist, and these we shall discuss and resolve. But I want to make it quite clear that the aggressors are the imperialist-colonialists, first because they are the alienators of our lands to which we do not admit their right, whatever they are determine among themselves; and second, because they are the prime users of force, and if their international law was objective and not framed simply to legalise their loot, there would be no need for it. We are not out to take what is not ours, but we have a perfect right to fight for the birthright of freedom and the ownership of our land that has been filched from us and is being illegally withheld.

Inasmuch as our struggle for independence and our subsequent national and continental development is bound up with the question of peace, since our very survival hangs upon the decisions of the great nations, we once more put forward our appeal to them. Immeasurable quantities of money, not to talk of the futile waste of energy, brains and productive capacity, are put into the manufacture and explosion of the most lethal weapons of destruction that man has ever bent his ingenuity to devise. It is a fair comment on the state of Western civilisation that this should be regarded as its highest pinnacle of achievement, while millions of the world's populations in Asia and Africa, yes, even in Europe and America, exist on the fringe of bare subsistence. We still call upon the powers who hold the fate of mankind in their hands, to turn away from the production of these appalling means of mass destruction and to devote to peaceful uses the harnessed power of the atom. How excellent it would be if, instead of preparing for the destruction of mankind, one barest part of the means financing it, could be used in the rapid development of the less developed parts of the world, and thus destroy colonialist-imperialism forever. It is a sad reflection on the leadership of these nations that they should have within their reach the power for doing good and yet refuse to adjust themselves to the opportunity of making effective their ability for doing this good. I hope that before long sanity may prevail and that mankind will receive the benefits of the uncountable wealth now being catapulted into the atmosphere.

The question of peace, particularly as it affects African independence and development had related to the United Nations, the great world organisation which despite all its shortcoming, is the international repository of the world's hopes. Some time ago this organisation showed such nervousness in the implementation of its own decisions and resolutions over the Congo that the small nations began to wonder whether it cold be effective in their protection and if confidence should be reposed in it. Its vacillations caused the death of one of our bravest fighters—our brother Patrice Lumumba.

The Congo is perhaps one of the most glaring examples of how the neo-colonialists use the most machiavellian means to continue their imperialist depredations, by turning to their contrivance the ambitions of power-thirsty politicians and tribal divisions. Belgium, we know, never prepared her colonies for independence, and when she transferred power to the Congolese people, it was obvious that it was never intended that independence would be genuine. Because of the lack of political organisation in the Belgian Congo as a result of the colonial policy forbidding it, and the hurried attempts to forestall nationalist cohesion by encouraging tribal associations, the ground was well set for the interfering tactics of the imperialist and cold war interests that entered Katanga to guard their investments and sever it from the jurisdiction of the central government.

If we need an illustration of the use to which tribalism can be put by the divide and rule tactics of imperialism and its African puppets, the Congo provides it most graphically. Unfortunately, Patrice Lumumba was not allowed time to complete his unifying policy, and was put out of the way precisely in order that he might not do so. Everything that followed from the neo-colonialist and cold war strategy in the Congo and the manipulation of strings in the United Nations by the same interests, is testimony to the crying need for African unity everywhere and in everything that is done in Africa.

I am glad that at the time Ghana did not withdraw her troops from the Congo, like so many other nations, as this would have left the way wide open to the interventionists who were only waiting for the opportunity to be left alone to take over this enormous territory for themselves.

Now I come to the task directly of the fighters who are in the front rank of the struggle. Unity, fellow Freedom Fighters, must be the watchword of those who are leading the masses into the battle for independence in the many parts of Africa which, alas, are still under the dragging yoke of colonialism. You must close your ranks and stand firmly together. You must forget your theoretical differences and minor political polemics. The forces that are massed against you, as I have explained, are mighty indeed, and though they have their differences in many things, they are united in their determination to keep Africa as their rich economic province. Division among us is a luxury we cannot afford. Our open squabbles are the advantages which the enemy loses no time to exploit and thereby decimate our forces, and undermine our purpose. This is an aspect that we must examine most seriously so as to find means of clearing away such differences as we have, and coming together in a solid phalanx, to meet the enemy on a common front.

Moreover, the sectionalism of separate organisations within a single territory, for instance, apart from its fissionable dangers, is wasteful in the extreme. The endeavour to enlist mass support for a multiplicity of organisations avowedly dedicated to the attainment of independence can only lead to tribalist and religious communalism, on which so many good intentions have foundered. It provides greater opportunity for the employment of imperialist divide and rule tactics. It creates a diffusion of much-needed organisational manpower, which could be more tactically deployed if encompassed within a single organisation. Furthermore, a single organisation could embrace the whole popular support and channel its enthusiasm around one programme, instead of dividing its attention and its allegiance to the disadvantage of the struggle. Sometimes the impression is created that in certain places the struggle is for leadership *per se* and not so much for independence. This is unfortunate, and I say it with grief and reluctance. It is regrettable when some leaders appear to be more concerned with being leaders than with understanding hat we are leading for and what we are leading against.

I hope that I have made clear to you here the nature of the struggle as I see it. As I have said, it is our African struggle, and it is taking place here in Africa. Many of our Freedom Fighters have been forced out of their countries as a result of the militant part they have played in the struggle, and they are continuing to play their part in many different ways. But they will understand me when I say that the struggle for the independence of each territory will, in the final analysis, be fought out within that territory. Therefore, the freedom fighters outside must keep their links with those at home and be guided to some extent by the closer knowledge of the state of things of those who have been left to carry on behind. Moreover, they must not be surprised if other new leaders are thrown up in the course of battle, as it will not always be convenient for those at home to wait upon the word from the exiled leaders. What you have to do here is to examine all the aspects of your struggle and forces within and without and plan for the final assault. The struggle may be long. It will certainly not be easy, and you must not allow yourselves to be deflected by such extraneous issues as border differences and other contentious disputes which can have no relevance as long as your independence is in doubt, and which will disappear within a unified Africa. What you must be prepared to defeat are the designs of the colonial powers to divide up your territories so as to deprive you of portions that are essential to your viability and economic development.

It is a common practice for the colonial powers before they finally transfer power to look around for some means of partitioning the subject territory, in order to weaken it and force it back under their neo-colonialist wing. You must be prepared to meet all such devices. Just as in the course of battle you must look for and learn to recognise the agents and the provocateurs whom the enemy sends out to infiltrate your ranks as a fifth column. There may be among us spies and informers for the enemy, betraying their own people for a mess of pottage. Worse than these are the agents who come to us with honeyed words to weaken our discernment in discriminating the true purpose behind the facade of friendship.

We must be prepared for many dissembling of this kind and others. You will be warned against this and independent state. You will be flattered, cajoled, denigrated, lauded. They will pit you against each other, against the independent states. They are already classifying your enemies and your friends among us by dividing us into the Casablanca and the Monrovia states.

Speaking for myself, I must state that this classification is insidious and designed by the neo-colonialists to crystallise a permanent division in the ranks of African leaders. They identify the Casablanca group as radical and militant, and the Monrovia group as moderate and reasonable. This division is a vicious thrust at African unity and the sooner we realise its danger and counteract it, the better it will be for all of us.

Let us tell the colonialists, and neo-colonialists, that moderate or radical, militant, or reasonable. Africa is Africa, one and indivisible. It is not their business to categorise our attributes. That is for our African masses to do, and they will do it in a manner that will spell unity and not division.

We must quickly throw a bridge across this and other artificial openings which the imperialists are trying to create between us. We cannot do this by fulfilling the parts assigned to us by them or by associating with our ex-colonial masters in a rider-horse relationship.

It is for us to bring nearer the day when we shall be able to refer to ourselves simply as the African power and give to our detractors and traducers evidence of our determination to be rid of imperialist classification and nomenclature.

This is all part of your task, fellow Freedom Fighters, as it is ours, the already independent states. The destiny of our peoples, the fate of our great continent, lies in your hands. You have to your credit a most impressive list of successes in the grim struggle for independence. The face of Africa is changing, physically, socially, and mentally. Before you, Comrades, lies the task of putting the finishing touches to complete the picture of a fully liberated Africa, united, strong and forward-looking.

May the deliberations of this conference of nationalists Freedom Fighters place the final nails in the coffin of colonialism and neo-colonialism in all their forms and manifestations, and imprint the seal of freedom, unity, progress, peace and prosperity on our people and on Africa.

Keep aloft, Freedom Fighters, keep aloft the fighting banner. Africa demands that we keep on fighting until victory is won. Now is the time to fight. Now is the time to win. Long Live African Independence ! Long Live African Unity ! Long Live African Freedom Fighters !

15

OPENING OF POLICE HEADQUARTERS

June 9, 1962

LADIES AND GENTLEMEN,

The magnificent building which we are opening to-day gives concrete evidence for all to see that the Government is determined to provide our Police Service not only with the best possible working conditions but also with the necessary facilities for the maintenance of the highest possible standards of efficiency and good conduct in the service.

The reputation of the Ghana Police Service to-day is very high and we are proud of that reputation. No doubt our Police had its own colonial mentality. In the past its fond slogan was *Betule ya che* and the attitude of the Force was one of subservience to the colonial master.

I am happy to note that this attitude is now radically changed and that the Police have the same slogan as other national institutions, namely, "SERVE GHANA NOW".

It is gratifying also to know that the human material which now enters the Police Service is improved admirably. Persons with secondary education and even graduates are finding their way into the Police Service. This augurs well for the nation, as it is important that our Policemen should be well informed and be capable of balanced judgment.

A Police officer—indeed, every Policeman—is first and foremost a servant of the State and a friend of the people and his life is one of continuous service; faithful, unquestioning and loyal service. We have every right to expect therefore that all our Policemen will dedicate themselves to their work, will be courteous but firm in all their dealings with the public, and will give steady and unswerving loyalty to the State which is theirs to protect. The Police must be vigilant at all times in the interest of national security.

I wish to place on record the fact that our Police Force has, over the years, played a truly memorable role in our task of nation building. It has achieved a high standard of efficiency in the performance of its duties and in the protection of our citizens.

A policeman's life is not an easy one. Indeed sometimes it is even dangerous. We therefore expect from our Policemen the highest standards of courage, particularly moral courage, at all times. Every Policeman at some time or another finds himself exposed to the temptation of bribery of some sort. But, he is a poor Policeman indeed who succumbs to such temptation. We are all determined to see that bribery and corruption are eradicate completely from the fabric if our social life. Corruption can undermine our industrial and social development and destroy the drive to raise the living standards of our people.

Our Policemen are the main instruments in the detection and destruction of the evils of bribery and corruption. Policemen should therefore not allow themselves to be contaminated by these evils, but must build up and maintain a reputation of integrity and honesty for the Police Service. Our Police Service must be incorruptible. One of the factors on which is based the strength of the State is the incorruptibility of the Police and the Army. The stability of the State and the strength of the Government depends also upon popular will and mass support since the police are the representatives of the Government whom the mass of the people need in their everyday lives, their relationship and popularity with the public is of the utmost important.

Many visitors to Ghana receive their first impressions of our people from the Police whom they meet on arrival. It is only natural therefore, that such persons, judge our nation by those first impressions. Our Police must remember at all times to conduct themselves in a manner that upholds the service of the good name of Ghana.

During the past few years, at the Police Service has expanded considerably and grown appreciably in overall strength. I am aware, however, that in view of the rapid technical, economic and social advances being made by this country a further expansion is necessary in order to ensure that adequate police services are available to the community. It is thus the policy of my Government with the establishment of village Committees and District Councils, to provide Police Services throughout the country, so that every village shall have its own "village policeman".

The efficiency of any Police Service depends, to a large extent, on mobility and the existence of adequate facilities for communication. This is a matter to which I have always attached great importance and the Police Service has therefore been provided with the Armoured Car Squadron, a highly mobile, operational unit which can deal with any threat to Internal Security, promptly and effectively. It has already proved its operational value in several trouble spots and has been a marked deterrent to crime generally.

Progress in the other branches of the Police Service has been equally satisfactory. As late as 1947 Police transport at any Station was limited to one solitary vehicle popularly known as "Go Inside" Since the Party came into power, however, it has tackled the question of Police transport very vigorously, and as a result the strength of this fleet has increased more than fourfold in the last few years. Highly efficient mechanical workshops exist to provide maintenance facilities, and a considerable amount of workshop equipment has been bought this year.

We have a Police College, designed to train our officer Cadets for appointment in the Commissioned ranks of the Service. The Police College which I opened in temporary accommodation in 1959, is I am glad to say, now in its own permanent buildings.

We are happy to place the services of this College at the disposal of all other independent African States. Any of our sister countries which would like to send their young Police officers here for training, are most welcome to do so. This will make possible the interchange of ideas and experiences on the problems of crime detection and the enforcement of law and order which are common to all African States. There is a great advantage in training our Police officers locally, in that all matters that are not related to our particular problems can be eliminated, thus making for more concentrated effort and greater efficiency.

I believe that the Police Organisations of independent African States have a positive contribution to make towards the realisation of our goal of a union of all African States. Crime is international and knows no frontiers; and the establishment of a Continental African Police Organisation, parallel to the existing International Police Organisation, will not only facilitate the tracking down and apprehension of criminals and the dissemination of intelligence, but also contribute towards the progress of our effort in the direction of African unity.

What I would like to see is a series of regular conferences organised by the Heads of Police of all independent African States. The aim of these conferences should be to ensure and provide the widest possible mutual assistance between the Police Organisations of all African States and to establish and develop all institutions likely to contribute effectively to the prevention and suppression of crimes. I hope that our Commissioner of Police will take the initiative in this matter and play a positive role in organising the first of such conferences.

Ladies and Gentlemen, in declaring these buildings open, I wish to express the hope that all who will work in them will rededicate themselves to the service of Ghana. I also hope that these fine buildings will be a continual of inspiration to the Commissioner of Police and all those who work under him.

I have great pleasure in declaring the new Police Headquarters formally open.

16

OPENING OF BRITISH SCIENCE EXHIBITION

June 13, 1962

Thank you, Mr. High Commissioner, for what you have said and for inviting me to speak.

LADIES AND GENTLEMEN,

I am sure we are all happy to be here to see this Science Exhibition. I am informed that the exhibits which you will see represent many striking achievements of British scientists, not only in pure science, but also in the application of science to practical problems. These achievements are not only a credit to British scientists, they are a credit to scientists everywhere, for science is international, and refuses to be divided into national compartments. Whatever their nationalities, all scientists contribute to a common fund of human knowledge.

Scientists in the older countries start with many advantages. They inherit remarkable legacies and have at their disposal not only cumulative scientific experience, but also many facilities for their work. Scientific achievements, however, is not confined to these countries. As far back as the ninth century, the museum at Alexandria was a great centre of scientific research and learning, where mathematics, medicine and the physical sciences received serious attention. It would appear through that time has piled its dusk thick on this African achievement already. We now live in the twentieth century, the age of the atom, jet propulsion and journeys into outer space. We in Africa therefore require to carry out in a decade what it has taken other peoples and nations centuries to achieve. This demands a revolution not only in the existing political and social order, but also in the substance and structure of our education in order that we can keep pace with the swift scientific and technological advance achieved in other parts of the world.

Here at this Exhibition, we can see the development of practical ideas by scientists and technicians, in their endeavour to serve their nation, their fellowmen and the world community.

Ghana's need for scientists, engineers, architects, and skilled men generally is great. If we are to sustain our industrial and agricultural revolution, and contribute significantly to the progress of the African continent, it must be our clear duty to accelerate our pace many times over and improve existing training facilities for science and technical education. We must ensure that a lively interest in science is created in the children very early in their school life.

Our teachers will have to learn the importance of associating the work in the classroom with everyday life, so that the children realise that science is not something which works only in the laboratory, but is all around us in nature and in the things we see in our daily life.

The Government proposes, in this connection, to establish shortly a Science Museum. The purpose of the Science Museum will be to arouse and increase the interest of Ghanaians, young and old alike, in science and scientific techniques. The Museum will contain simple working models of machinery, and will provide an explanation of the scientific principles on which the models are based. There will be sections in the Museum also deals with the pure science explaining, for example, the nature of the universe and the structure of atoms in a lively and straightforward manner.

In the modern world it is necessary that everyone of us should understand the basic principles of science and technology. It is not enough to have some people trained as scientists. Everyone must have a basic understanding of the methods and achievements of science. This Exhibition, therefore, and the proposed Science Museum, can be regarded as educational projects of the first importance for Ghana to-day.

We are anxious to produce as quickly as possible the scientists and other trained men whom we require to assist in industrial, agricultural and technological programme. We believe that it is only on the basis of our progress, strength and prosperity that we in

Ghana can be in a position to help our fellow Africans in other parts of this continent. The purpose of the development of science and technology, the foundations of which we are now laying, is therefore, the peace, progress and welfare of our own people and peoples elsewhere in Africa and in the world. Many scientists to-day are working on research projects, the purpose if which is not the means of increasing the happiness and welfare of mankind, but primarily creating means of destruction, preparing new weapons and perfecting the fright weapons they have already invented. This indeed a terrible blot on the name of science. How can healthy, enthusiastic zeal for scientific knowledge survive in a country where a large proportion of the young men and women who take up a scientific career find themselves ultimately working for destructive ends? We in Ghana, and indeed in Africa, have a vested interest in peace and prosperity. We can assure every scientist working in Ghana or who wishes to come to work here, that he will never be requires to work for any purpose other than for the progress and benefit of mankind.

We hope that the negative aspect of science is only a passing phenomenon, and that it will soon be possible for the great powers to agree to put a stop to this unhappy development. The Government of Ghana together with men of goodwill throughout the world will continue to bend all its efforts towards, and support those policies which will bring about peace and prosperity to mankind.

But our efforts in this respect will be of no avail unless the great powers who have made such spectacular advances in scientific development realise the urgent necessity for mobilizing their efforts and resources entirely in the interest of peace. The present arms race in which the great powers are engaged is a serious threat to peace.

Are we, all the people of this globe, to be forever at the mercy of a handful of men who eye each other menacingly and suspiciously from the tops of their bomb piles? What is our lot if the tension proves too much and make just one of their number go berserk?

Not only do we call upon the leaders of the great powers to turn away from the use of scientific knowledge for the production of means of destruction, but we also call upon all scientists, whether their nationality, to refuse to sell themselves to agencies who cold use their knowledge for man's destruction. Let them have courage to bring sanity and order once more into this world. Their knowledge should be devoted to the promotion of human welfare and happiness. The inconceivable amount of money which has been used for destruction purposes could be used to wage war on disease, poverty and want throughout the world.

I hope that we shall go away from this exhibition with a keener appreciation of what can be achieved by man in scientific research and the application to peaceful and purpose of the fruits of such research.

And now, I should like to express my own appreciation that the Government of the United Kingdom has decided to mount this Exhibition. I hope that as many people as possible, especially our students and school children, will come to see it and learn something of what science has achieved for man. I look forward, in the not too distant future, to opening a similar Exhibition of Ghanaian scientific achievements.

Ladies and Gentlemen, I have very great pleasure in declaring this Exhibition open.

17
OPENING OF THE ACCRA ASSEMBLY

June 21, 1962

MR. CHAIRMAN, DISTINGUISHED FRIENDS OF THE ASSEMBLY,

You are meeting at a time when the United Nations Committee of eighteen nations at Geneva is still engaged in its task of attempting to draw up a treaty for general and complete disarmament. Anything that can be done to assist in this work is of the utmost importance to mankind.

Humanity is perched on he edge of a dangerous precipice from which one fatal miscalculation may bring mankind to the brink of annihilation. The Powers developing the atom bomb for war purposes claim that their actions are dictated by the instinct of self-preservation. Experience has shown, however, that the stock-piling of armaments as a basis for "negotiation from strength" is the very soil from which the seeds of war constantly break out. The old maxim—"if you wish for peace prepare for war"—is outmoded in our time. A serious peril stares mankind in the face. Who can save us from this peril? A voice—a bold and courageous voice resounding across the world with man's yearning for peace and calling upon the Nuclear Powers to end forthwith the stock-piling of nuclear weapons for man's destruction.

Let us hope, distinguished friends of this Assembly, that yours will be that voice, and that those who hold the fate of mankind in their hands will pay a timely heed to the sincerity and fervour of your voice.

You have assembled here not as representatives of countries or of political parties or organisations, but as individuals who are determined to save the human race from those who would condemn it to destruction. The fact that you have come here as individuals will, I believe, allow you to do that new thinking and make fresh approach which is to-day so essential to the survival of mankind.

A new approach to these problems and a new thinking on the issue of man's reservation is demanded. Out of this body of eminent thinkers who have actively concerned themselves with the welfare and progress of mankind must come a positive answer to that demand.

It is hope that by putting my point of view before you, I might be able, to some small extent, to assist in this fresh approach and new thinking, and it is in this spirit that I am now venturing to address you.

Morality

In thinking over the problems which you will be considering, what strikes me most forcibly is this. What the world to-day lacks is a code of international morality which measures up to its technological progress.

Tell the truth; Love your neighbour as yourself; Succour the poor and the needy; Waste not the bounty which nature and science have provided; Do no murder: These are the maxims of all religions and moralities and the principals which men try to apply in their private lives.

Can one honestly say that the nations of to-day try to apply these principals to international life?

Instead of the truth being told, whole peoples are deceived and led to believe the exact opposite of the truth namely, that by he use of shelters, or the like, many people could escape death in an atomic war. In reality, the survivors are likely to be confined to those engaged in directing and waging nuclear war, since those who think it terms of a "hot war" automatically accept that these are the only lives which must at all costs be saved.

Campaign of Hate

Ideological differences between the nations have unfortunately become the basis of a campaign of hate between peoples, and the whole apparatus of science is employed on both sides in this campaign. The result of this can only be the obliteration of the human race with all its achievements. The vast sums of money consumed in this campaign could be used to finance national and international programmes for the eradication of disease, poverty and want. It is believed that about One Hundred and Fourteen Million Pounds (the equivalent of Three Hundred and Forty-two Million Dollars) is spent every day—every single *day*, mark you—on the production of weapons of mass destruction.

Surely what we need is a public morality, which will teach that what is wrong in private life is equally wrong in international relations.

I say this because I believe that in the world of to-day no nation, great or small, will saved by its armaments. Not only the defence of small nations, but the defence of the greatest powers on earth, ultimately depends not on weapons of mutual mass destruction, but upon the collective conscience of mankind. If by coming here you can do something to arouse that conscience, then your journey will not have been in vain.

Peace: A Practical Policy

And let me say this: you have a great chance of success. It must be realised that in the world of to-day there is no longer that conflict between morality and national expedience which up till now has bedevilled any attempt to permanently solve international problems without recourse to war. Peace, disarmament and banning of atom bomb testing are to-day practical policies. The obstacle to their implementation is no longer based on the economic or political needs of national states. The obstacle is solely the persistence of that outmoded attitude of the mind which still regards war as a continuation of political policy by other means.

Let me illustrate what I mean by referring to the history of the abolition of slavery.

Nations as a whole never are able to abide by a moral code which, if respected, would seriously impede their economic well-being. In the days of slavery, irrespective of the moral code to which they nominally adhered, the master class continued to own slaves.

The pious slave-owner merely excused his activities by priding himself on treating his slaves more humanely than the his irreligious colleagues. He quoted Aristotle and the Bible to justify slavery.

Some of the bravest sprits of each of the past condemned slavery, but their voices were few and their moral appeal went unheeded for centuries. Then suddenly, so it seemed, that moral appeal which had for so long fallen upon deaf ears, touched men's hearts and, first the slave trade and then slavery itself, were abolished.

No Profit

Why this sudden change of attitude? Was it not because slave trading and slavery, though still a considerable source of profit to those who practised it, had ceased to be a prime economic necessity for the Powers of the day?

The abolitionists task still remained difficult and arduous as they had to overcome ingrained habits of mind, but it was no longer impossible and by courage and perseverance, they won their day.

I believe an almost exact parallel exists with the issue of war and peace in our own time.

Up to the moment of its abolition, there were still powerful forces who had a vested interest on slavery and who honestly believed that their country's way of life was bound up with slavery's continuance. They were prepared to fight and even to die in its defence. But their cause was lost once the mass of the people was made to realise that slavery was not only morally wrong, but that economic progress demanded its abolition.

In the same way there are today powerful groups who believe that only through armaments can their civilizations be preserved. But objective truth is not on their side. World war is no longer a practical economic policy. In this age, there is no single objective which can be gained though world war. Conversely, in this age, there is no single objective which cannot be gained by the peaceful use of the world's recourses.

In the old days of slavery, the abolitionists were regarded as unworldly idealists and cranks whose ideas were perhaps morally justifiable but which were quite economically impracticable. Looking back, we can see now that the exact reverse was the case. Those who believed that their civilization depended upon slavery were the impractical men, mesmerised by the past. The abolitionists were the realists.

New Doctrine of Hope

To-day, those who advocate disarmament, the abolition of the threat of nuclear conflict and the ending of the cold war, are the realists and history is on their side.

Therefore, you can not only stir the conscience of the world; you can teach a new doctrine of hope. It is because war has thus ceased to be an essential instrument of policy that moral opposition to it has a real possibility of success, particularly if it is organised and developed on the basis of hard practical argument, and upon the teaching of a new international morality.

This new morality should teach primarily a sense of individual responsibility. The menace of nuclear warfare could be removed tomorrow if every individual in every country was convinced that had a personal duty to prevent the destruction of mankind in an atomic holocaust.

At the moment, in my view, the greatest danger to peace is apathy. An attitude of mind exists among a great part of the peoples of many of the nuclear powers, or aspiring nuclear powers, that the issue of peace or of nuclear war is a matter not for them but for the politicians, the generals and the technicians. By propaganda they have become indoctrinated with the idea that the greatest issue in the world to-day, the survival of the human race, is not a question upon which they can act, but is something which must be left to s small group of supposedly military expects to decide. Such a view is not only untrue: it is immoral. The issue of peace and war in this nuclear age is the concern of every human being. The future of the human race is a responsibility no man or woman can delegate.

Stir World Conscience!

This is why I have said that this Assembly must therefore not only stir the conscience of the world, but establish a new doctrine of hope. For the nations which have accepted the Charter of the United Nations, war should no longer be an instrument of policy.

The menace of nuclear warfare could be removed tomorrow if every individual in every country acted as though he had a personal duty to preserve mankind from nuclear war.

What is true of individuals is also true of nations. Ghana is non-aligned, but we are not an island isolated from the world. We are a part of mankind and the fate which befalls mankind is the fate that will befall us. Ghana's policy of non-alignment is not a policy of neutralist detachment. No more than the ostrich, will we find safety by burying our head in the sand and pretending to be unaware of what is around us.

The people of the world, therefore, have a duty to carry on a positive campaign to awaken the conscience of the world, to secure the banning of atomic tests, the destruction of all weapons of mass slaughter and the reduction of conventional armament.

Join the Crusade

If this campaign is to be successful, the men and women of all countries throughout the world, including the scientist, the leaders of religious faiths and the writers, must work to influence public opinion and to arouse the conscience of mankind against nuclear war.

Above all, the humble people who are to be found in every country upon earth and who believe in the dignity of the human race, and who realise that man was not created to destroy himself, and that mass suicide is the most deadly of all sins, must join in this crusade.

In ridding the world of the threat of nuclear warfare, vehement protest is an essential ingredient in arousing man's conscience. I should like to express my admiration and respect for those among you here, and to all those others who cannot be with us to-day, who have led such protest. I admire the courage of scientists, religious leaders, writers, and others who have braved scorn, and often persecution, for speaking out boldly against nuclear warfare.

Economic Suicide

We must convince the bulk of mankind that nuclear war is not only against all morality, but is economic and political suicide for all who attempt to base their policies upon it.

We must show that world war has no longer any economic or political justification and that the things which it is supposed might be gained by war can, in fact, be gained only by peaceful means.

For this reason, I am particularly happy that this Assembly contains a number of individuals skilled in economics and politics, and who have given detailed study to the technical problems of disarmament. It is by marrying their technical knowledge to the moral force of those who have protested against nuclear warfare that we shall find a solution.

Co-operation

I am delighted to see participants from so many different parts of the world. No country has a monopoly of ability and it is therefore of the utmost importance that those from the countries of Europe and North America should confer with distinguished men and women from Africa, Asia, Latin America and Australia. We should by no means underestimate the effect on world opinion of the view of the non-aligned individuals and nations from these four continents. If a common policy can be put forward by them, it would have a decisive effect.

Success or failure in your task will, I believe, depend on how realist a manner you tackle the root causes of the conflicts of interest in the world to-day. In other words, we must, if we are to create a "World without the Bomb", understand the conditions which have created "The World with the Bomb."

In my view, the tensions which have produced the "World with the Bomb" can be divided into roughly four classes.

Critical Analysis

First, there are the tensions resulting from the problems left over the Second World War.

Secondly, there are the tensions arising out of the striving of the peoples of the less developed parts of the world to better their future and throw off the burdens of imperialism, colonialism and racial discrimination.

Thirdly, there are tensions resulting from a conflict of ideologies.

And fourthly, there are tensions caused by the possession by some powers of weapons of mass destruction.

However, before beginning to criticise the policy of those Powers whose actions have led to the "World with the Bomb," it is always most important for States and individuals to bear this in mind. We have neither the responsibility nor the experience of conducting the policy of the nuclear powers, and therefore we cannot say for certain how, if we were placed in their position, we would act. In making any criticism it is right for us to remember that we have been spared the weight of responsibility that rests on their shoulders; each one of us should say himself, before condemning any policy: "There but for the Grace of God might go I".

Second World War

Let me now deal with the first of my point—the tensions resulting from the problems left over from the Second World War. The very fact that peace is to-day threatened by tensions created by the Second World War underlines the point that world war cannot solve our difficulties. The victors in a world war, by their very victory, create problems which contain the seeds of a new war.

USSR, A Power: US Industrial Might

The lessons of the last two Great Wars teach, above all else, the uselessness of world war in the conditions of to-day. Indeed, the consequence of these last two wars have been the very opposite of what either victor or vanquished anticipated when they entered the conflict. Looking back on the First World War, its two most important consequences can now be seen to have been the establishment of the Soviet Union and the building up of the industrial might of the United States of America. Both these events have since profoundly affected the world for good, but they were neither aimed at, nor even anticipated, by those who went to war in 1914, and in fact both worlds, in all probability, have occurred in any event without the senseless mass slaughter on the battlefields.

In the same way, the outcome of the Second World War was the direct opposite of anything intended by the aggressors or indeed by any of those who first joined in the conflict against them.

Movement for Colonial Freedom

Looking back on this last war its most dramatic result was certainly never anticipated by those who entered in 1939. Its most important consequences was to set in motion a train of event which led inexorably to an irresistible movement for colonial freedom. A great part of the globe previously under colonial domination has, within less than a score of years since the end of the Second World War, become free.

This, coupled with the establishment of socialist states ion China and Eastern Europe, has profoundly affected the balance of power in the world in a way never contemplated in 1939. In consequence, in the post war period, the Great Powers were confronted with problems for which they were unprepared, and this has added to the tensions in Europe which the war provoked.

Berlin

Foremost among these is the German question which has been no more settled by the Second World War than it was by the First. It is another example of the futility of modern war that those powers which, in unity could fight the war, cannot to this day—seventeen years after the war has ended—agree among themselves on the terms of a German peace treaty. This is converting the German question into a potential source of a third World War.

At the moment the German issue is high-lighted in the Berlin problem. It may seem strange that a city so remote from Africa should be a central question at an Assembly in Accra. We must however discuss it, if only because a war over Berlin would engulf the whole world. It is therefore right that we ask at this Assembly why cannot this problem be solved?

So far as I can see, there is substantial agreement between the great powers on three major points.

First, both power blocs are agreed that there should be no nuclear weapons in Berlin; secondly, that there should be no increase in the number of the military units now stationed there; thirdly, they appear to agree that access to West Berlin should be internationally guaranteed. In fact the dispute over Germany boils down to whether or not the East German authorities should or should not supervise the passage through Berlin territory of the internationally guaranteed traffic. In other worlds, the world is threatened with nuclear was because the Great Powers cannot decide who should stamp whose passport on the route to Berlin.

Anyone who studies the detailed documentation of this Assembly must be struck with how few points in fact divide the Great Powers when these are compared with the points upon which they are agreed. It seems to me that one of the tasks of this Assembly might be to isolated these points of disagreement and then boldly suggest possible solutions other than those already advanced by either of the power blocs.

A Crisis of Confidence

In so doing, however, it must be remembered the no solution, however reasonable, will in fact be acceptable unless a way is found to resolve the basic distrust which keeps the Great Powers apart. Fundamentally, what we face is not a difference on details but a crisis of confidence.

My Government has sponsored this Assembly because we believe that it is in meetings such as this a beginning may be made to resolve this crisis of confidence.

In the same way as one may argue interminably as to which came first, the chicken or the egg, so one can argue interminably which comes first in the control and inspection of disarmament. Both sides are agreed that there should be inspection and control over disarmament. The difference arises as to whether there should be inspections and control over the armaments which remain after disarmament.

Distrust versus Spying

As I see it, this cannot be resolved because the Western Powers will not accept the Socialist bloc's estimate of arms which remain unless there is inspection, and the Socialist bloc will not accept that any inspection team examining existing armaments will not be, in practice, a spy organisation.

Such a crisis of confidence can be resolved by a bold stroke.

I believe that an impartial inspection team cold be found and that its very impartiality would reassure both the Socialist States that it was not a spy organisation and the Western Powers that the Socialist countries were not in fact retaining more armament than they said. One task of this Assembly, so it seems to me, is to make positive proposals as to how such an inspection team could be constituted.

Let me come now to my second point—the tensions arising out of the striving of the peoples of the less developed parts of the world to settle their future and to throw off the burden of colonialism, neo-colonialism and racial discrimination.

Change Bound to Come

In my view, this Assembly must face the fact that the less developed parts of the world are in a change. One of the great values of this Assembly is that it contains eminent and experienced individuals from all over the globe. They, I believe, may be able greatly to assist in arriving at possible solutions for one of the most difficult of questions, namely, how to reconcile the maintenance of balance of power between the Great Powers with the need for change in the African Latin American and Asian continents.

Philosophy of Historically Imperative Force

May I give you one example: Ghana has been much criticised for not condemning as aggression the Indian action in using armed force to end Portuguese colonialism in India. Fundamentally, the basis of this criticism was that real non-alignment means the support of the status quo. Can such an argument be supported by history? Was Garibaldi an aggressor when he fought to unify Italy? Were the British and United States Governments wrong when in the early nineteenth century they made it clear that they would oppose by force any attempt by Spain to reconquer her lost South American colonies? If the United Nations had been in existence in the year 1776, would we have expected those countries who were non-aligned at that date to have condemned France for coming to the aid of the American colonies then in revolt against Britain?

Goa—Moral Arguments Fail

In Goa, force became the only remedy only because the United Nations was unable to end colonialism on Indian soil, and only because moral arguments and political pressure were of no avail. Yet those who, like Ghana, accepted this action as proper, have been accused in the words of one critic "of the tacit acceptance of the dangerous doctrine of good and bad wars".

This is an issue we must face. A study of history shows that there has never been a conflict in which each side did not believe that they were acting in accordance with justice, and indeed, in which they did not evoke Divine Providence to support their arms. "Praise God and pass the ammunition", was their cry. Once one accepts the conception that a was is permissible, the door is opened to every type of conflict.

What is the answer?

I believe it lies first in a positive policy being adopted by the United Nations. The United Nations cannot survive as an organ dedicated to preserving the existing order of things.

If an injustice is universally recognised, as it was for example, in the case of the continued Portuguese occupation of Goa, then the United Nations can only avert military action by initiating peaceful change.

O Yes, No Power Can Stop It!

The world is going to change. No power on earth can stop it, short of destroying all humanity. The choice before us is, therefore, peaceful change or change brought about by force. No international organisation, however powerful, can stop the clock of history. I am a strong believer in peaceful change. In the Positive Action campaign which I initiated in Ghana during colonial times, and which led to a realisation by the British authorities that the time had come to end colonialism here, I always insisted upon non-violent action.

Where Peace Fails . . .

I am, however, sufficiently a realist to understand that change cannot always, at every period in history, be brought about by non-violent action. It is no coincidence that every single one of the five nations to whom permanent seats on the Security Council are allotted have had their revolutions or rebellions, which they look back to with justifiable pride and upon, which, indeed, their present constitutions are based.

The fact is that in certain periods of history the masses of the people in some particular country have no other means of escaping from a regime which is intolerable to them except by armed revolt. We must accept this fact and we must also accept the fact that the forces which produce a revolution, a revolt against colonialism or a movement for national unification, can occur at any point of time in history.

History Shows . . .

For example, what took place in Britain in the seventeenth century, in North America and France in the eighteenth century and in Latin America, Germany and Italy in the nineteenth century, is to-day, in our own century, taking place before our eyes in Africa.

One of the great difficulties of our age is that peace has become equated with compulsory political stagnation. The theory of balance of power results in this or that States being arbitrarily assigned to the zone of influence of one or other of the great power blocs.

False View

In consequence, any attempt by the people to alter the regime, whether it be by democratic or revolutionary means, is regarded not, as it should be, as a purely internal matter, but as an attempt to alter the balance of power between the power blocs.

It is unrealistic, however, to hope that the people most intimately concerned will see the issue in this light. Oppressed peoples in a less developed country, made desperate by tyranny and corruption, are not going to be deterred from getting rid of an objectionable government on the ground that it might upset the balance of power between the Great Powers. People struggling to free themselves from colonial oppression are going to get help wherever hey can find it. People artificially divided in the interest of the balance of power are going to continue to strive for reunification, and those suffering from racial discrimination are going to end it irrespective of the interests of those Powers.

The Argument that Holds No Water!

It is utterly unreasonable for the Great Powers to say to the less developed countries: "It is true we revolutionised our social systems. It is true that some of us executed our kings and emperors in the name of liberty, but this was a luxury to which we were entitled and to which you are not. You must bear all your present misfortunes because otherwise you will upset the balance of power on which we depend for our safety."

We must be realistic and understand that such a policy is in fact impossible. We must accept change, even violent change, in the less developed countries of the twentieth century.

Liquidate Colonialism!

The highly developed countries of the world of to-day must realise that before they could become fully developed they had, in fact, to go through an exactly similar process. General and complete disarmament must presuppose complete and total liquidation of colonialism.

Let me now turn to my third point: the tensions arising from a conflict of ideologies.

Conflict Within Conflict!

I should have thought that history, at least, has taught us the futility of ideological wars. When we look back, for example, upon the great conflict between Christianity and Islam, what positive benefit to humanity was secured by it? It deprived the Christian world of the benefit of Arab science and agricultural techniques and set back for perhaps four hundred years the technological and industrial development of Europe. It imposed on the Arab world a militaristic pattern which in the end destroyed the splendid early flowering of Islamic science and culture. The Christian world, which at the time of the crusades, believed that it was fighting for a clearly defined ideology, was soon to discover that Christianity itself—which had appeared to them as universal monolithic faith—was capable of splitting into rival ideological groupings which fought the most bitter wars against each other.

Survival

To-day the religious faiths, at least, have learned that co-existence is essential if any religion is to survive. The lessons of history have shown that no faith can prosper if it attempts to impose its tents by force of arms upon those who will not, of their own free will, accept its teachings. To-day, as the composition of this Assembly shows, it is possible to bring together people of the most diverse faiths in order to discuss the problems of mankind. Indeed, the wheel has turned the full circle and the most eminent religious leaders now consider that their faith demands of them that they meet and discuss with others of quite different religious persuasions the questions which must be settled in order that mankind can live a full and happy life.

Example and Argument, Not Force

In an age of nuclear warfare we cannot wait for that long period of time which had to pass before the religious faiths realised the importance of living together in peace with those who believed in conflicting ideologies. We must make the world realise here and now that ideology can only be imposed by example and argument, and not by force.

You do not make a man change his opinion by killing his fellow countrymen with an atom bomb, any more than you can alter a man's secret religious beliefs by burning his co-religionists at the stake.

The Power to Choose

If religions can to-day co-exist, why cannot nations which have different economic and political theories as to how the state should be organised, do the same? To me at any rate, co-existence does not only mean that the two power blocs will agree to tolerate each other; it also means that every nation both great and small shall be entitled to choose and follow the path best suited to itself.

Clear-Cut

Let me illustrate what I mean by referring to the problems of the African continent.

The unity of Africa, which is to me and to many others, the most important single international issue, may follow from either the system of capitalism, as practised in the United States to-day, or the system of socialism, as practised in the Soviet Union.

To say this does not of course mean that those who think in these terms condemn either of these two systems, or suggest in any way that they are not suitable for the countries in which they are practised.

Since, however, owing to Africa's colonial background, there is no class of indigenous African capitalists, it is impossible to build up a capitalist system in the same way as, for example, Japan has done. A capitalist system in Africa upon the United States model, if it could be constructed at all, which is doubtful, would be essentially a system of the domination of Africa by foreign capital.

On the other hand, we have throughout Africa, indigenous institutions as, for example, our traditional forms of co-operative undertakings n agriculture and commerce, which provide us with a basis upon which we can build. But in order to do so we must construct social and political systems of our own type and it would be quite unrealistic to think that this could be done by adopting wholesale the economic and political systems of the Soviet Union.

Leave Us Alone!

We wish to learn from the capitalist and the Socialist systems. In so far as is practicable, we want to adopt to our own circumstances what is best in both of them, but we are not prepared to be forced to say we belong irrevocably to either camp. Unfortunately, this is often what the Eastern and Western blocs attempt to force us to do. They accept the view that he who is not for them wholeheartedly is at heart their opponent. This is not true. All that we wish to do is to live in friendship with all countries of the world, irrespective of their political ideologies. All we ask in return for our friendship is that we are left alone to work out our own destiny.

The emerging States of Africa do not present either a military or an economic threat to any other nation. Why, therefore, must we become the battleground of rival ideologies?

At present there are crying evils calling out for remedy in Africa. These can be solved by the African peoples themselves without any threat to the peace of the world, but unless the African people are allowed to deal in their own way with these evils, sooner or later they imperil the peace of the world

Remember Congo

Monstrous injustices, such as racial persecution, and in some colonial territories the virtual enslavement of a great part of the population, will not be for ever endured. Unless they can be remedied peacefully, they will erupt into war.

The Congo is a proof of the danger to peace which the Great Powers involvement in Africa entails. The Berlin Conference which partitioned Africa was called, it should not be forgotten, because of the first of the Congo crisis. This crisis was solved by neutralising the Congo, so far as the Great Powers were concerned, by handing it over to the King of the Belgians as his personal property.

After Bomb, Colonialism will still Threaten Peace

The failure of such solutions as these are to-day plain for all to see. King Leopold's regime was one which shocked even a world that accepted the principals of 19th century colonialism. It left behind it a legacy of racial hatred and military brutality which has borne bitter fruit in our own day. The Belgian regime was neither able to maintain its power nor to provide the machinery for a peaceful transition to Independence. Because certain Powers considered that in 1960 they has the same right again to settle the Congo problem in accordance with their own ideas, the Congo situation almost produced another World War. Divided and weak as the independent African States still are, it was their intervention, supported by non-aligned countries, and using the machinery of the United Nations which saved the day.

The Meaning of Neo-Colonialism

It is true to say that even if the threat of the atom bomb were removed, world peace would still be in jeopardy. This is so, because world peace is intimately bound up with the liquidation of colonialism. As long as the question of colonialism remains unsolved, world peace will still be threatened.

The colonial powers while handing over independence, see to it that the substance of domination through economic power is maintained. This conduct is extremely dishonest and leads to unnecessary complications and crises.

On the 1st July next, Ruanda Urundi become free as separate independent States. The two territories could have been easily united but that was not in the interest of the Belgians. But the record of the

Belgians in the Congo fails to be a warning to themselves. Their intention to grant independence while retaining actual control over Ruanda Urundi, appear quite clear from the pronouncements and gestures of Belgium in her desperate anxiety to keep Belgian troops in those countries after independence, on the pretext of helping to maintain law and order.

It is the same story which produced the Congo crisis, that Belgium wishes to repeat. She must not be allowed to do so, and the United Nations must avert another catastrophe in Ruanda Urundi by resolution and firm action.

Balkanisation

The greatest danger facing us is the balkanisation of Africa into States too small to maintain real independence, much less to expand their economies and be able to stand on their own feet. The example of Latin America is before us. Balkanised Africa, like the Balkans in 1914, could constitute a political tinder box which any spark could set alight and involve the whole world in flames. The struggle for African unity and independence is therefore an essential part of the struggle for world peace.

Co-existence and disengagement run together. The Great Powers cannot co-exist and at the same compete for spheres of influence in the less developed parts of the world.

Disengagement

It may therefore be of value to you if I explain in a little detail how I envisage disengagement on the African continent.

Obviously there are many difficulties to be faced. Disengagement is impossible so long as former imperial powers retain in practice control over their former colonies. In the case of a number of African states, the former colonial power continues to control the Civil Service and the administration generally. It has a strangle-hold over the economy by maintaining its control of the central banking system. Further states have created which are so small as not to be economically viable, and these countries in fact are compelled to depend upon their former colonial rulers for subsidies in order to meet the ordinary expenses of administration. Under such circumstances, of course, there can be no disengagement as the former colonial power in fact retains every attribute of government except for the purely nominal attitude of sovereignty.

Even where the former colonial power does not retain this degree of control, there may be an indirect control exercised in order ways.

For example, African independence is quite incompatible with the control of the African economy by expatriate finance capital.

Anti-African Foreign Firms Will Lose Investment

A way must be found by which this capital can continue to be used in Africa and give a fair return to those supplying it, and yet be used within the framework of a policy formulated by the people of Africa and designed to promote their well-being. The details of such a change are no doubt complicated but surely this general principle is clear. Ultimately, any foreign firm which works against the African people will lose its investment. Ultimately, any foreign firm which works in partnership with the African people is bound to share in the prosperity which our economic expansion will bring.

African Trade Unions—Stop the Strings

Disengagement also involves the cessation of ideological pressure. For example, both the capitalist and the socialist countries are agreed on the value of Trade Unions, and they both believe that Trade Union organisation should include an international organisation. Unfortunately, they cannot agree on the composition of that international organisation, and in consequence there are two rival bodies both claiming that they are the only true world organisation of trade unionists.

How can we possibly build a strong trade union movement in Africa if we are under continuous pressure to join either one or other of these rival groups? We want fraternal assistance from trade unionists from all over the world, but we want it without ideological strings attached to it.

So long as international trade unionism is based upon rival ideologies and cold war politics, it is impossible for African States to link their trade union system with either group. External pressure to join this or that grouping does nothing to help trade unionism in Africa. It merely divides the African people, and divided peoples are in themselves a threat to peace.

This trade union question is merely one example of the type of pressure which creates instability in Africa. Much more serious is the ideological assumption that Africa is merely an extension of Europe. In Africa we regard with sympathy and understanding the desire of European nations to achieve a closer union and establish a Common Market.

Dividing Africa to Unite Europe?

But why must it be necessary to divide Africa in order to unite Europe? If a Common Market for Europe is the right policy, why should there not be a Common Market for Africa? The plans for a European Common Market, however, as at present formulated, contain proposals for perpetuating the old unnatural pattern of colonial trade by which commerce was not on an inter-continental African basis but was almost exclusively between the imperial power and the colony.

The Blunt Fact

The colony produced the raw materials, the cash crops and the minerals, whose price was in effect determined by the importing monopolists of the imperial power. In return, the colony had to receive the manufactured goods of the imperial country, paying a price which in practice the commercial interest of the imperial power could dictate. This may or may not have enriched the imperial power. It certainly kept the colony in poverty.

It is essential to realise that the continuance of such a system is in itself a threat to world peace. Colonial revolts are not only occasioned by the desire of a people to control their own political government. In fact, they are more often produced by economic oppression. British rule was tolerated by the American colonies so long as it was not accompanied by economic oppression. The American War of independence, the first and certainly the most significant of all colonial revolts, arose directly from the economic fetters imposed by the imperial power on the thirteen colonies.

Grave Danger

If the European powers use their present economic strength to impose a similar system upon their ex-colonies, sooner or latter the relationship will become intolerable, and there will be a peoples' revolt against the neo-colonialist regime. Since such regimes are backed by military pacts with the former imperial power, such a revolt would assume at once an international character. There will then arise the grave danger that the State or States in revolt against neo-colonialism would follow the classic pattern set by the American colonies, and call in outside powers to give them aid, which in many states has strings attached to it.

Unity—Africans Ready!

For this reason alone, I believe that it is in the interests of world peace for all the Great Powers to disengage themselves from Africa. This, of course, will not solve all our problems. African unity, which is the prerequisite for solving both the economic and the political problems of Africa, can only be created by Africans. It is a task whose magnitude I in no way underestimate, but it is one which we must undertake ourselves and which we cannot expect other nations outside our continent to do for us.

No Interferance

All that I propose is that the Great Powers hold the ring and agree among themselves not to interfere in our affairs. If only they do this, whatever happens on the African Continent can never be a threat to world peace.

What I am proposing may sound novel and revolutionary, but it is in fact nothing new.

A Leaf from European History

In 1860 the unity of Italy was only secured because Britain made it known that she would oppose by force any attempt by outside powers to interfere with the internal revolution which swept away those small States which had for so long been the main cause of Italian poverty and backwardness. Indeed, history provides a number of examples of occasions when the Great Powers have isolated conflicts by agreeing among themselves to enforce a policy of genuine non-intervention. It is, of course, most necessary that a non-intervention policy is properly and genuinely enforced. History unfortunately also contains examples—as, for instance, in the Spanish Civil War—when the principle of non-intervention was used as a cloak for intervention. This misuse of the principle of non-intervention should not deter us from attempting to apply it in a proper way. It should, however, serve as a warning that non-intervention, if it is to be effective, must be most strictly supervised. In such supervision, non-aligned countries, in cases where their interests are in no way bound up with the particular matter at issue, must play an important part.

There is a grave danger that where non-intervention is enforced by one states and an area of the world is thus isolated from outside pressure, this can develop into s form of intervention. For this reason I believe that disengagement should not be organised through the United Nations and should not be imposed by any one Power declaring that it will not permit outside intervention in a particular part of the world.

Stop Under-Cover Support!

If there is to be disengagement in Africa, it is essential first that the Great Powers do not give under-cover support to colonial regimes.

To one practical example : Portugal, one of the principal remaining colonial powers in Africa, has a European population which is only about a million and a half greater than that of Ghana. It is one of the poorer European countries and in fact the gross National Product per capita of European Portugal only exceeds that of Ghana by Twelve Pounds per head. Nevertheless Portugal maintains a vast colonial empire. Her Africa territories alone, are twenty-three times the size of European Portugal and the colonial peoples whom she rules over greatly outnumber the inhabitants of Portugal itself. It is obvious that Portugal could not maintain such an empire in the face of rebellion by its colonial subjects without outside assistance. The Powers which to-day provide Portugal with assistance against the Angolan people are giving hostages to fortune. Obviously and naturally, those who are fighting Portuguese colonialism must ultimately be tempted to seek similar assistance from rival power blocs.

On the other hand, if the interested Powers agreed to give no further support to Portuguese colonialism on the basis of an agreement that no other non-African power would intervene, Portugal would have to negotiate. I believe that arrangements could be made by which Portugal would not lose financially through a peaceful transfer of power. Even if she did, provided those powers who to-day assist her to maintain her military forces supplied the sums of money for the peaceful development of Portugal itself as they now spend on supporting her tottering colonial empire, Portugal would be much better off economically, and much more stable politically than she is to-day.

Supplying Arms

The Great Powers cannot have it both ways. They cannot on the one hand supply finance and arms to a colonial power which would otherwise be forced to negotiate with its colonial subjects so as to secure a peaceful transfer of power, and then blame the Africans in revolt for endangering world peace by resorting to arms.

South Africa is a typical example of this. Though the Security Council has declared that racial discrimination in South Africa is a threat to world peace, some permanent members of the Security Council are to this day quite openly supplying arms and building armament factories for those who are practising racial discrimination in its most brutal form.

South Africa Cannot Long Endure

Does anyone here believe that a regime so fundamentally evil as that of South Africa can for long endure? But when it goes down in chaos and civil war the blood of many innocent men, women and children will be on the heads of those who have so irresponsibly armed the oppressors of the African people.

There is one more argument for disengagement from Africa. Colonialism not only oppresses the colonial people; it ultimately corrupts imperial power itself.

The imperial powers of the nineteenth and early twentieth centuries were caught in this dilemma.

"One Man One Vote"

At home they were democracies built on the principle of "One man one vote," but they could not obviously adopt this political principle in their colonies, and they therefore invented in its stead the theory that by natural right there was an "elite" who were entitled by reasons of their supposedly superior education and qualities to rule, irrespective of the views of those over whom they ruled. countries where there was a European settler class, they naturally became the "elite."

This theory, so convenient for maintaining colonial domination, spread back from the colonies to the home country itself. The colonial "elite" allied themselves with their corresponding class in the imperial power and ultimately claimed the moral right to dictate policy not only in the colony but in the home country as well.

OAS and French Bomb

Algeria is the typical example of the final effect of this colonial ideology in practice. A completely irresponsible minority group in Algeria actually believe that they have a moral aright to dictate the policy of France. and in order to do so, to commit any atrocity which they see fit.

This situation presents an acute danger to world peace. The O.A.S. in Algeria have managed to possess themselves of most of the types of weapons used by the French army, and they employ them indiscriminately against the civil population without the least regard for the international consequences of their acts.

Can you wonder that Ghana and many other African States expressed the most extreme concern at France's atom bomb testing in the Sahara and her desire to become a nuclear power? What would have been the fate of the world if one nuclear bomb possessed by France had fallen into the hands of the O.A.S.?

That Infinitesimal Northern Rhodesian "elite"

It is not only in France, however, that colonial policy is dictated by a European "elite" The total European population of Northern Rhodesia, if transferred to Britain, would not be sufficiently large to be entitled to be a constituency to elect one out of the 360 members of the British House of Commons. So ingrained, however, is the colonial ideology of the "elite", that when these same persons are living in Northern Rhodesia, it is accepted by politicians who practise democracy at home, that they are entitled, if not to control the government, at least to have an equal share in it with the two million Africans who comprise practically the entire population.

Disarmament and Disengagement

I have dealt at some length with the African situation because naturally it is the problem with which I am most familiar; but I would not have done so had I not thought that it illustrates admirably the need for combining a policy of disarmament with a policy of disengagement.

At a pre-Assembly meeting at Zagreb early this year, some of you who met to plan the work for this Assembly, suggested that there might emerge from it an Accra Plan. I hope, if it is possible to formulate such a plan, that those working on it will consider the need for disengagement without which I believe peaceful co-existence is impossible.

No Bombs, No Bases!

In regard to Africa, I should like the continent to become not only a non-nuclear zone, but also a zone where no foreign military bases are allowed. I should like this to be paralleled with an ideological truce and an agreement not to try to convert Africa into an economic appendage of any other continent.

Keep Out Cold War

Africa should not become a battleground for the cold war. The cold war and the cold mentality should be kept out of Africa. It is in the interests of world peace that this should be so.

Such a plan for disengagement would, of course, apply equally to many parts of the world. In Laos, both the United States and the Soviet Union have now agree that the only possible solution is a neutralist regime. The main obstacle, however, to the establishment of such a regime was he strength of the two rival ideologies which have been encouraged by the rival power blocs

Mistrust and Mutual Fear

Surely we can profit by this example and provide for disengagement before it, of necessity, has to be proved in a civil war.

It is unnecessary for me to deal at any length with my fourth point, for it is abundantly clear that mutual fear, which is at the root of so much of the mistrust in the world to-day, cannot be eliminated so long as the Great Powers are in a position at one stroke to annihilate each other. It is of course for this reason that your detailed discussions on the methods and processes of disarmament is of such great importance. Further, disarmament is essential if the productive forces of the world are to be released for use in developing the less developed areas of the globe. The mere fact of so using these resources would do much to destroy these dangerous tensions to which I referred under my third head, and which arise out of the disparity in wealth and opportunity for economic advancement between the more developed and the less developed countries.

"I Protest!"

This Assembly has been named "The World Without the Bomb." It is ironic that it should be meeting at the very moment when nuclear devices are being exploded. The experts on these matters among you will be able to tell you what military value, if any such tests have, but however great such military value may be said to be, I should still protest against them irrespective of who is the testing power or where the tests are undertaken.

When the major nuclear powers refuse to heed the universal appeal to stop the manufacture and testing of nuclear devices, do they imagine that the rest of the world resigns itself submissively to what protection it can get from fall-out shelters? Unfortunately for mankind, it does not. One by one, country after country begins to think hopefully in terms of defence. Slowly but surely learn how construct these lethal weapons for themselves and, with much pride, they boast them into the atmosphere. Yesterday it was France. To-day, maybe, it is Australia. Tomorrow it could be Japan, China, Italy, India, Pakistan, Greenland and many other countries determined not to be left behind in the arms race.

The Grave Warning

Apart from the great danger of fall-out from all this testing one wonders just how nuclear fission our globe can take before it—before our whole planet, indeed, is itself split into millions and illions of tiny particles and blasted into eternity.

Does mankind, I wonder, really understand where he is heading or?

No matter how small some people think the world has become in his age of jet propulsion and astronauts, it is still big enough to contain us all happily and peacefully, communists and capitalists, Mohammedans, Buddhists, Christians and Jews, Black skinned, yellow skinned and white skinned. For those who cannot reconcile themselves to this idea, who convince themselves that the globe is now small to accommodate their various ideologies, I would recommend that they get together in one of their man-made satellites and take a good look at the globe from outer space. In that vast expanse of either, looking down on our world and around at the thousands of other possible worlds, how can any man presume to have the right or the power to interfere with the all-powerful mechanics of the universe?

Scientists, Please Hands Off

Finally I would like to make an urgent appeal to every scientist, to every man and woman, whoever they are and wherever the live, to disassociate himself from everything connected with the manufacture, testing and stock-piling of nuclear weapons.

I would like at this juncture to venture a suggestion which, on the face of it, may sound a little naive, but which I think might serve to increase our awareness of the vital part we can play in speedily bringing about nuclear disarmament.

World Without the Bomb Association

I wonder whether the distinguished members of this Assembly might, during their discussion here, consider forming and launching a club or association with world-wide membership, to be called, perhaps, "The World Without The Bomb Association." Each member could be given a badge which he should wear at all times so that he can be identified as an active participant in the nuclear disarmament campaign. Membership should be restricted, of course, to those who are both morally and physically dissociated from the manufacture and testing of all nuclear weapons of destruction.

And the World Looks On . . .

We have reached a point where each one of us must decide, once and for all, whether we want to live—and by living, I mean living normally and happily, without any kind of threat of destruction hanging over our heads—or to be destroyed in an atomic war. On this issue of disarmament or nuclear destruction, we cannot listen to politicians, to generals, to our leaders and our superiors: this is one time when the individuals, the ordinary men and women of the world, must face the situation themselves and when they must have the supreme courage to do what they know is right. Whatever this may cost us, it is after all, a small price to pay to save mankind from annihilation and to restore sanity, peace and order to the world. Let us have the courage of our convictions and let us act to-day.

Courage: Akwaaba

Mr. Chairman: It has been a great honour for me to address you, and on behalf of the Government and people of Ghana, to welcome you.

People in many lands are looking up to you for some new hope and some new light in these perilous times which try men's souls.

Distinguished Friends: I thank you for listening to me and I now leave you to your task.

18

SECOND ANNIVERSARY OF REPUBLIC

June 30, 1962

Tomorrow is Republic Day—the second anniversary of the glorious birth of our new nation as a Republic. On this occasion, however, our celebrations will be a somewhat limited scale and they will not include the usual formal ceremonies like the Military Parades, which I know you all enjoy. I hope that the provision of permanent stands at the Black Star Square will be completed in the next few months, and that it will again become the scene of our national functions and parades.

I have come to the Studio on the eve of this occasion to salute you, and to share with you some thoughts about our nation. Tonight, there will be general merry-making in the cities, towns and villages throughout Ghana. It is only right hat we should rejoice because we know that Republic Day signifies for us the day of real independence—the day when our nation become really free and sovereign.

The past year has not been easy for any of us. We have had our share of the general slump in world prices, and this affected our main source of income—cocoa. As a result, all of us have had to tighten our belts in an effort to prevent any disruption of our economic life. I am glad to say that we have succeeded in this regard and to-day our economy is strong and as buoyant as ever.

Many attempts have been made by our detractors to misrepresent out intentions and motives, to put obstacles in our way, and to hamper the realisation of our national objectives and progress. On every occasion, however, our people have risen like one man and foiled these attempts. I do not propose to make any specific mention of any particular occasions, but you are all aware of the events which led to the detention of the people a majority of whom have recently been released. All of us now have the opportunity to help in rebuilding our nation.

We have a double role to play. Our first duty is to build Ghana as a first-class nation. This demands the greatest effort on our part to ensure the implementation of our policies at home. At the same time, Ghana has an over-riding duty to keep flying the banner of the national struggle against imperialism, colonialism and neo-colonialism in Africa. These are the two paramount national obligations which we must discharge.

In fulfilment of our promise to continue the struggle until the whole of Africa is liberated, Ghana has consistently been in the forefront of that struggle. This has earned us the enmity and hatred of those countries which have a vested interest in colonialism. Notwithstanding this, we remain undeterred and we are ever determined to pursue this struggle until victory is won. Africa is our birth-right and no sacrifice can be considered too great for us to bear in order to make her free, respected and restored to her rightful place in the world.

As I speak, Ruanda and Urundi are on the eve of independence. This is a great thing for Africa, and our own celebrations here are doubly reinforced when we consider that our efforts in the interest of our brothers elsewhere in Africa constantly bear fruit. When some months ago we met freedom fighters from Ruanda-Urundi at the Kwame Nkrumah Institute of Ideological Studies, we knew their independence was near. We take this opportunity, therefore, to offer our hearty congratulations to our brothers in Ruanda-Urundi. In the name of African unity we wish them success in their new life.

Five years ago when we called the first Conference of Independent Africa States, only eight African nations were free. By tomorrow, that number will rise to thirty-one. This is a tremendous achievement for Africa. But the struggle still continues. Africa will indeed be free and united.

I referred earlier to our two paramount national obligations, but I must say that there is a third duty which is of equal importance. It is the part that we can play in the struggle for world peace. We, as a nation, together with other African countries, have a highly vested interest in peace. We need peace to enable us to develop and repair the damage done to us through centuries of imperialist rule and colonialist exploitation. We cannot therefore afford the risk of another world war.

The Accra Assembly which has just ended is an eloquent testimony to the desire of mankind for peace, and I feel sure that its results will be welcomed by all those who are truly interested in peace and in welfare of mankind.

There has recently been a certain amount of loose and irresponsible talk about the state of our reserves. It is true that owing to our programme of industrialisation and mechanisation of agriculture we have had to use part of our reserves to finance the purchase of industrial plant and equipment. Even so, our reserves now stand at over seventy million pounds sterling, which by any consideration, and having regard to all our circumstances, are quite substantial.

Friends and countrymen, we look forward to the future with courage and confidence—confidence in ourselves and confidence in our party and Government.

No one who looks back to the condition of our country as it was five or six years ago, can fail to realise the tremendous achievement that has taken place in every sphere of our national life. Tema Harbour, constructed at a cost of twenty-seven million pounds, which was recently opened, is still being expanded. The new township which has already cost over ten million pounds is also being developed as a first-class modern city. More houses have been built and basic services such as roads and water have been provided in all parts of the country. All these developments have been provided for entirely from our own resources.

The national progress and prosperity of Ghana is the concern of every citizen. We must, each one of us, play our part to make a success of our national programme. Let us determined here and now that we shall, by our own exertions, keep Ghana on the road to prosperity and strength. The days are gone—and gone for ever—when we were prevented from playing any role in the affairs of the Government and when we thought, therefore, that we had no responsibility for the welfare of the country. We now had no responsibility, and we owe it to posterity to discharge it faithfully and well.

I wish you all a happy Republic Day.

Goodnight.

19

OSAGYEFO'S PEACE AWARD

CEREMONY OF THE
AWARD OF LENIN PEACE PRIZE

State House
July 2, 1962

MR. SKOBELTZYN, LADIES AND GENTLEMEN,

I am touched by the honour that has been conferred upon me by the award of the Lenin Peace Prize for 1961 and I accept it in all humanity. I regard this award not only as an honour to me and the people of Ghana, but also as a recognition of our modest contribution towards the promotion of world peace.

The man after whom the Peace Prize is named and commemorate—Vladimir Ilych Lenin—is one of the most outstanding personalities of this century. Indeed, his like is rare among men. He grew up with the conviction that revolution and ethics theory and practice, are inter-related. Revolution was always for him a moral issue for the realisation of social justice. He believed that a society founded on the exploitation of man by man was immoral and must be changed. Lenin was a man who devoted himself to the cause not only of the Russian people but indeed of humanity. In this pursuit he succeeded in establishing a new social system that has made a remarkable impact on the course of world history.

Throughout his life Lenin strongly believed that the surest way of securing enduring peace was by the abolition of all injustice and social inequalities. Lenin was deeply loved by the Russian people and today thousands from all over the world file past his embalmed body in the Mausoleum at the Red Square in affection and reverence to this great man who made Socialism a reality. To him "man's dearest possession is life, and since it is given him to live but once, he must so live as not to be besmeared with the shame of a cowardly existence and trivial past, so live that dying he might say, all my life and my strength were given to the finest cause in the world—the liberation of mankind."

Today the preservation of peace should be the concern of us all. Here in Africa we see the problem of peace in two main dimensions. First, we see it in terms of its international repercussions. In this light the problem of peace centres mainly on the removal of the threat of war. Secondly, we see the problem of peace in terms of the liberation, reconstruction and unity of Africa. As I have often stated, there can be no peace in the world until imperialism and colonialism are abandoned and not tolerated as instruments of policy in international relations.

I believe that the spirit of man can triumph over physical might. I also believe that there is a moral order in the universe and this moral force, this power of right over might, will ultimately overcome the evils of oppression, exploitation and man's inhumanity to man.

Fear and hatred will be removed from the hearts of men and the frontiers of peace will be greatly extended. Mankind must make a conscious efforts to break t he crisis of civilisation and in which man's essential humanity is in danger of being overwhelmed by the power and influence of man's inventions.

The scientific and technological achievements of our time have raised man to a new plane of existence in which the fruit of man's labour can create a better and happier life for man.

The same achievements have, so to speak, contracted the world into such a small span that we have become each other's next door neighbour. We must therefore learn to live together in peaceful co-existence. I am confident that the nations can co-exist irrespective of different social, economic and political systems. Co-existence can be realised and buttressed by a selfless policy of disengagement, and the practice of secular democracy which ensure the complete separation of all forms of religious from the State, and the pursuit of man's cultural and spiritual development.

This medal which has just been pinned to my breast represents a moral force generated by the burning desire of people of all nations for peace.

Mr. Chairman, I am grateful to the International Lenin Peace Prize Committee for this honour. I accept the award on behalf of myself and the nation which I have the privilege to represent as President.

20

THE ELEVENTH PARTY CONGRESS

Kumasi
July 28, 1962

COMRADES,

The last annual Party Congress took place in 1958 at Koforidua and under very different circumstances. Ghana was then a Dominion. Today we meet as citizens of the Republic of Ghana, exercising our sovereign rights in the best interests of ourselves.

Our great party, in the meantime, has undergone serious changes in its structure and organisation, and what is more, it has set the country on the road to socialist reconstruction. In this exercise some of us have fallen by the wayside by the weight of our own conduct. We who have gathered here today must have cause to rejoice that we have withstood the tempest of these trials and changes and have survived.

Our party's aim is all-embracing, inspired and dedicated to the people and Nation. We have stated often and made it clear that our objective is a one party state, which gives equal opportunity to all the people and distinguishes citizens for merit and achievement but not privilege.

This Eleventh Congress of our great party being held in this historic city of Kumasi, is unique in many ways. In a sense, it is the party dividing line between the past and the future, between what we have achieved and what we plan to achieve. We must therefore mark the importance of this occasion by positive decisions.

When we met in 1958 at Koforidua, the National Headquarters of the party secretariat was accommodated in a small office in Kimberly Avenue in Accra. The general staff numbered less than thirty. The office was poorly equipped and the administration was a sort of stop gap arrangement. We launched a building appeal fund. Party members and friends generously subscribed. The result is the magnificent headquarters building of the National Secretariat which now imposes its gorgeous personality on the scene around George Padmore Road in Accra.

The Party Administration was re-organised and streamlined, both at the centre and in the Regions. Sixteen departments were set up to cater for various aspects of Party activity. The Party now employees over two hundred full-time officials at National Headquarters and in the Regions. No one who visits our National Secretariat can fail to be impressed by the effective and efficient arrangements for serving not only our Party members but also the general public.

One of the most successful exercise carried out by the Party during this period was the change of membership cards. The Central Committee decreed a change in membership cards and directed that new cards of a simple design be issued. The cards were distributed on a basis whereby every member had to obtain his membership card from his branch Party. By this method floating membership is eliminated. Today every single party member belong to one branch or another. Our membership, not taking account of supporters and sympathisers, stand at two and half million.

In 1961, major change took place in administration. I assumed office as General Secretary of the Party and Chairman of the Central Committee. I did so in response to the invitation of the Central Committee to me, to take up the post in order to give personal direction to Party administration.

Our youngmen, imbued with a spirit of dedication and service, are thronging by the thousand to the colours of the Party. Looking at them, I am sure that Ghana has a bright future in human material. Our young generations, led by the Young Pioneers, will grow up with the slogan "Ghana First" on their lips and give of their best to Ghana in honest work and honest living.

The Party organisation is effective in all its sections and the Party integral bodies—the Trades Union Congress, the United Ghana Farmers Council, the Co-operative Movement and the National Council of Ghana Women—are all active and doing good work.

I am aware that hard work still lies ahead of this Party and that we must try to allow our continued success to make us over optimistic. It is only human and right, however, that we should congratulate ourselves on our achievements so far. The danger lies in complacency. As long as we do not rest on our oars, as long as each Comrades realises the importance of "carrying on", the Party will keep on its path of success.

I have frequently pointed out that here in Ghana, and for that matter in other parts of Africa, political action must be taken all along the line for as long as possible. The ravages of colonialism and imperialism are such that only political action based on proper political considerations and direction can effectively repair the damage. That is why it is most important that the party should be in a position to give essential leadership to all national action, at all times.

This demands that the Party leadership must be well-informed and its actions well considered. The party has therefore built at a great cost, the Kwame Nkrumah Institute of Ideological Studies at Winneba. Its object is to give party ideological education. Deserving activities, as well as those comrades who are interested, are given opportunity to gain ideological training in theory and practice and to advance their knowledge in other aspects of Party education. Many successful seminars have recently taken place at the Institute and more and more Comrades are becoming interested in the work of the Institute.

The Party must keep faith with the nation and work hard to provide full employment, good housing and equal opportunity up to the highest level for educational, spiritual and cultural advancement for all the people. Our task therefore is to build a socialist state, an equitable and progressive social order in which the condition for the development of one is the condition for the development of all.

This means a reconstruction crusade led by the Party. The National Executive and the Central Committee have therefore given the most careful consideration to the agenda for this Congress and decided that our main work should be the consideration and adoption of the Party Programme for Work and Happiness and the approval of the Party revised Constitution.

The Programme has been widely circulated throughout the country. It has been discussed and explained at Party rallies and meetings and by the newspapers and the radio. Opportunity was given not only to Party members but also to everybody to study and criticise, thus fulfilling our promise to the masses that no action would be taken on the Programme until the people had fully expressed their views on it, thus giving effect to the general policy of the Party that the masses should be consulted in all our actions.

I must report that we have received criticisms and suggestions in this regard but that by and large, the nation overwhelmingly support the programme and by resolutions, telegrams, letters and other means, demonstrated its will for Congress to adopt it for implementation.

I do not find it necessary to comment here on the contents of the Programme. Surely delegates must have studied its provisions before now since the Programme has been in the hands of the public for several months. It deals with varied subjects covering the whole of our national life including Tax Reform, National Planning, Banking and Insurance, Forest Husbandry, Animal Husbandry and Poultry Production, Fish Production and Marketing, Industrialisation, Agriculture, Education, Culture and Leisure, Transport, etc.

The Central Committee put considerable work and thought into the draft programme. It is prudent therefore, not to dismiss any provisions lightly.

The amendments to the Constitution are straightforward and not complicated. One major amendment deals with the establishment of Party Special Branches. It provides that special branches of the party shall be established in working places. The purpose of these special branches is to study and propagate the principles of Nkrumaism, Party decisions, policies and programmes. Already most of these special branches which are not chartered branches have actually been established and are doing very useful work.

It is important for Party members to realise that the Party Constitution is the fundamental law of the Party and therefore the protector of all Party members.

Party Comrades, for their own sake, should endeavour to acquire a good working knowledge of the Constitution. In this way, their rights and duties will be clear to them and their conduct will be properly guided by it at all times. Apart from the protection that the Party Constitution gives, Party members can also protect themselves by their own integrity and honesty. I have in recent times spoken so mush on this subject and I have emphasised this point very clearly both in the Dawn Broadcast and in my Address to the National Executive at the Ideological Institute at Winneba, the subject matter of which has been printed and forms the Guide to Party Action. Delegates who have not had copies of the Guide to Party Action can obtain these at the Congress Secretariat. This great Party is deeply rooted in he people. The masses swear by it. Its prestige is reflected in the confidence reposed in it not by Ghanaians nut also by Africans elsewhere. The Party therefore has a duty and an obligation to stand by the people. Our performance must be first-class. Our sincerity must be above suspicion and we must always have the courage of our convictions. To achieve this, we have periodically to examine ourselves critically and to establish a firm discipline. In future we shall even be more critical of our conduct and actions.

As Comrade delegates know, we are embarking upon a period of intensive industrialisation and the mechanisation and diversification of agriculture. This is the time, therefore, when we shall need every available hand. The intelligentsia, the workers, the farmers and peasants, all the people must pull together in one great effort to liquidate and abolish all the remnants of evils of colonialism—illiteracy, disease, poverty, hunger, mal-nutrition and squalor. All the people must work together, for our interests are one and inseparable and our destiny in one and single.

It is good to note, in this connection, that more and more of our intelligentsia are finding their way into the Party and identifying themselves with it. It is time they identified themselves with the masses.

Ghana is based with some of the greatest assets and attractions any country can offer. Ours is a secular democratic State. We have no knowledge of inter-race tensions. We accept all colours, creeds and religions. Our mineral and agricultural potential is great. Our *per capita* income is comfortably high and our economy is buoyant.

We can make Ghana a showpiece of African success if this Party gives correct leadership to our people.

Hitherto development action has been taken on the surface. The places at the base have been little affected by the extensive changes taking place. The Party has therefore decided to re-organise local government in order to get action down to affect the life of the people at the base in their homes and villages. New districts have been created bringing up the number of districts from seventy to about hundred and fifty. It is intended that a district shall not only constitute a local council area administered by a District Commissioner but shall also constitute an electoral constituency. In addition there have been created town and village committees so that the internal life of villages can be substantially administered by the villagers themselves. The ordinary worker, farmer and peasant thereby becomes an active participant in the government of the country and the life of the community generally becomes organised right at its base.

All this work needs a steady party machine and administration which in turn need money for upkeep. Comrade delegates will realise that our party has no sources of income. It does not engage in trade or business. It depends solely on its membership, that is to say on dues paid by Party members and donations. We must therefore find more effective ways and means for collecting membership dues and donations.

Expenditure on the National and Regional Secretariats per month, amounts to almost twenty thousand pounds. We need a steady income of approximately two hundred and fifty thousand pounds annually therefore for running the Party's Administration and maintaining an effective political machine. This amount can be raised without much difficulty if every member pays regularly his dues of only three shillings a year. The Central Committee will request Finance Committee to work out new methods of collection to ensure that all members pay their dues as a duty to the Party.

The Party and Government have, during these years, worked tirelessly for a rapid economic transformation to catch up with our political advance. We have achieved much in the field of actual development and this is dealt with in outline by the Party. Ghana has maintained a steady progress since independence. Considering that these are our formative years of nationhood, we can afford to look at the future with confidence.

I have often pondered on the plight of most of our people in regard to social security. Surely citizens of Ghana must have the right to maintenance in case of sickness, disability, old age or some other handicap. Now only a few people in the service of the nation enjoy such rights. We must look at this matter with new eyes and plan an elaborate scheme of national insurance and pensions which would cover all the people. For example, imagine the lot of Party officials now, were some to suffer severe and protracted illness or some disability which prevented them from being able to work any longer—it could be a very sad and hard lot, for the Party would not be in a position to give such officials the adequate provision which would be necessary for their upkeep. This illustration is also true of many public workers. Such a state of affairs is rather undesirable and can work considerable hardship and misery on our people. I invite Congress to pay particular attention to this matter and urge the introduction of social security and national insurance schemes for all our workers people as quickly as possible.

It is incumbent upon this great Party to plan comfort and happiness for our old people. Old age could be a blessing if the aged can have succour necessary to keep themselves and their peace of mind. Unfortunately, most old people are often poor and since they get no income from any source whatever, their days end in sorrow and misery. We must correct this at all costs. Many of the aged must have rendered useful service of one type or the other to the state at some time and they must not be forsaken in their last days. Social Security should also provide for loss of bread-winner pensions, vocational training for disabled persons and maintain institutions for health, rest and leisure.

As you all know, this Party cannot achieve all that it has achieved without efficient organisation. Right from the start the Convention People's Party has always placed a premium on organisation, for organisation decides everything.

We have passed through trials and tribulations. We have

weathered fierce storms and upheavals in the young life of the Convention People's Party.

Comrades, a serious development is beginning to take place on our national scene. You all remember the cocoa politicians and the considerable havoc they caused with their seasonal activity. Every cocoa season they went about fabricating stories about offer of high prices of cocoa. They spread incredible and fantastic stories so as to deceive and confuse our common folk. Every cocoa season the Party and Government fought hard to counter these treacherous activities until the truth was established and the cocoa politicians disappeared with their inevitable doom.

Now a new traitor of the Nation has appeared. He is even worse than the cocoa politician. He is what I call the Budget politician. This vicious person goes about when budget time approaches, spreading all sort of fabrications about cost of commodities telling lies about the Party and Government and thus causing alarm and despondency among the people.

We must declare war upon these rascals and if they are in the Party, weed them out ruthlessly. If they are without, we must mercilessly and ruthlessly crush their activity and render them harmless, and like the cocoa politicians, send them to their inevitable doom. I charge all Party members to report to the authorities of any person or persons found indulging in this shameful and unpatriotic practice.

The Party and Government will launch a ten-year electrification scheme. Since we have placed our national emphasis on rapid industrialisation, it is essential that we should build electric power to the point where the smallest nook and corner of Ghana can obtain electric supply readily and cheap to facilitate activity.

The Government will also launch a seven-year development plan on a scale unprecedented in this country. From the North to the South, from the East to the West, Ghana will buzz with life and activity. Prosperity, progress and happiness shall stretch out before our people.

It seems clear from all this that our duty is to exert eternal vigilance, organise the Party more effectively in all its sections and ramifications and place it on a pedestal of achievement and supremacy. I know that in this matter we have a unanimous voice and a united will.

Comrade delegates, on behalf of Central Committee and the National Executive, I now have very great pleasure in welcoming you to this Eleventh Congress of our great Party, and placing before you the revised Constitution and the new Programme of the Convention People's Party.

21
AFRICA'S GLORIOUS PAST

OPENING OF THE FIRST INTERNATIONAL CONGRESS OF AFRICANISTS

December 12, 1962

DISTINGUISHED SCHOLARS,

It is an honour and privilege for me to welcome you to Ghana and to this First Africanist Conference. Your meeting here, within the ramparts of an African university, is a reflection of African's recovery and re-awakening. It is also a recognition of he new spirit which now animated the people of this great continent. It is even edifying that this Congress is taking place on African soil. I know that you who have gathered here represent various fields and branches of learning; in fact I see familiar faces of professors of universities and academics. What has impelled you, Distinguished Scholars, to gather here at such a time as this? You are here and are united by the fact that you want to find out the truth about Africa and, when you have found out, to proclaim it to the world.

Scholarly and academic interest in Africa is not a new venture. The desire to know more about Africa has been expressed from the very earliest times, because Africa has been the question-mark of history. To a Roman pro-consul: *Semper aliquid novi ex Africa.*

From the imaginings of the ancient geographers, an inaccurate and distorted picture of Africa often emerged. South of the Atlas ranges, a sandy desert was believed to extend indefinitely, with here and there a providential oasis, a rivulet, which nibbling and corroding its way through the sandy wastes, dripped into the sea. Even so, the ancients had some genuine knowledge of the African Continent, for they had a scientific curiosity about it. Thus Erastostheses and Aristotle knew that the cranes migrated as far as the lakes where the Nile had its source. And both of them thought that it was there that the pygmies dwelt. Among the travellers of the ancient world who tried to explore Africa, we may recall men like Strabo and Hanno of Carthage.

After these early travels, foreign knowledge of Africa became static until a new impetus was given to it by the Arabs and the Chinese.

The Arabs and the Chinese discovered and chronicled a succession of powerful African kingdoms. One of these kingdoms was that of Ghana, the pomp of whose court was the admiration of that age—and also of ours. It bred and developed within its borders the instruments of civilisation and art; its palaces were of solid architectural construction, complete with glass windows, murals and sculpture, and thrones within the palaces were bedecked with gold. There were other kingdoms such as those of Shonghay, Sala, Berissa, the renowned empires of Bornu, Wangara, Melli. The historians tell us that these empires and kingdoms were maintained with remarkable efficiency and administrative competence. Their splendour was proverbial in mediaeval times.

The Chinese, too, during the T'ang dynasty (AD. 618-907), published their earliest major records of Africa. In the 18th century, scholarship connected Egypt with China; but Chinese acquaintance with Africa was not confined to knowledge of Egypt only. They had detailed knowledge of Somaliland, Madagascar and Zanzibar and made extensive visit to other parts of Africa.

The European exploration of Africa reached its height in the 19th century. What is unfortunate, however, is the fact that much of the discovery was given a subjective instead of an objective interpretation. In the regeneration of learning which is taking place in our universities and in other institutions of higher learning, we are treated as subjects and not objects. They forget that we are a historic people responsible for our unique forms of language, culture and society. It is therefore proper and fitting that a Congress of Africanists should take place in Africa and that the concept of Africanism should devolve from and be animated by that Congress.

Between ancient times and the 16th century, some European scholars forget what their predecessors in African studies had known. This amnesia, this regrettable loss of interest in the power of the African mind, deepened with growth of interest in the economic exploitation of Africa. It is no wonder that the Portuguese were erroneously credited with having erected the stone fortress of

Mashonaland which, even when Barbossa, cousin of Magellan, first visited them, were ruins of long standing.

I have said that the pursuit of African Studies is not a new experience. But the motives which have led various scholars to undertake these studies have been diverse.

We can distinguish first a true scientific curiosity. Most of the Persian, Greek and Roan travellers exhibited this motive. Even when, as in the case of the Romans, they had a primary military purpose, they still tried and often succeeded in preserving some sense of objectivity.

Arab explorers were also often unbiassed in their accounts of Africa, and indeed we are grateful to them for what they wrote concerning our past.

By the time the European writings on Africa got under way, a new motive had begun to inform African Studies. Those early European works exchanged the scientific motive for one that was purely economic. There was the unbalanced trade in ivory and gold, and there was illegitimate trafficking in men for which these writings needed to find some sort of excuse.

The point I wish to make at this stage is that much of European and American writing on Africa was at that time apologetic. It was devoted to an attempt to justify slavery and the continued exploitation of African labour and resources. African Studies in Europe and America were thus at their lowest ebb scientifically.

With the abolition of the slave trade, African Studies could no longer be inspired by the economic motive. The experts in African Studies therefore changed the content and direction of their writing; they began to give accounts of African society which were used to justify colonialism as a duty of civilisation. Even the most flattering of these writings fell short of objectivity and truth. This explains, I believe, the popularity and success of anthropology as the main segment of African Studies.

The stage was then set for the economic and political subjugation of Africa. Africa, therefore, was unable to look forward or backward.

The central myth in the mythology surrounding Africa is that of the denial that we are a historical people. It is said that whereas other continents have shaped history and determined its course, Africa has stood still, held down by inertia. Africa, it is said entered history only as a result of European contact It history, therefore, is widely felt to be an extension of European history. Hegel's authority was lent to this a historical hypothesis concerning Africa. And apologists of colonialism and imperialism lost little time in seizing upon it and writing widely about it to their hearts' content.

To those who say that there is no documentary source for that period of African history which pre-dates the European contact, modern research has a crushing answer. We know that we were not without a tradition of historiography, and this is so, is now the verdict of true Africanists. African historians, by the end of the 15th century, had a tradition of recorded history, and certainly by the time when Mohamud al-Kati wrote Ta'rikh al-Fattash. This tradition was incidentally much, much wider than that of the Timbuktu school of historians, and our own Institute of African Studies here at this University, is bringing to light several chronicles relating to the history of Northern Ghana.

Of these chronicles, the most exciting traced down to date, appears to be the Isnad al-Shuyukh Wa il-ulama, written around 1751 by al-Hajj Muhama Ben Mustafa who lived in Western Gonja in Ghana. It gives details of the conversion of the Dynasty in 1585.

A great deal of interesting work has been done and continues to be done in learned centres in Africa. In Nigeria, for example, Dr. Dike has worked on Politics and Trade in the Niger Delta. Here, he reflects, like other Africanist scholars, a new African-centred approach to the study of the relations between the Delta states and Europe in the 19th century. In this connection, the collaboration of archaeologists, historians and anthropologists, studying different aspects of the history, institutions and culture of pre-colonial Africa, has produced beneficial results.

A large collection of manuscripts and other evidence helping this adventure has now been made in many African centres of learning. At the University of Dakar, for example, I understand that a great deal has been collected in the way of documentary material relating to the history of the Western Sudan. In Mali, also, considerable work is being done on pre-colonial history and the Museum at Bamako has gathered a great deal of material both useful and fascinating.

In Guinea, too the story of the contact between Europe and Africa is being written as an African experience and not as a European adventure. Similar work is being successfully undertake in the Ivory Coast. In Upper Volta, there is the important work of Professor Ki-Zerbo on the Moshi Kingdom, and has for some months now been working happily and successfully in our Institute of African Studies as an expression of the cultural unity of Africa.

In the East, a great deal of progressive work continues to be done. Documents and inscriptions in Eg'ez and Amharic, in Swahili and Arabic, in Old Nubian and Meroitic, are being collected in order to make possible our authentic reinterpretation of our past.

In Sudan, in Ethiopia, in Tanganyika, in Somalia, Kenya, Uganda, everywhere in Africa, there is purposeful effort to bring to light those means which alone will enable us to present our history as the history of the African people, the history of our actions and of the ideology and principles behind them, the history of our sufferings and our triumphs, This Congress, among other things, is an attempt to share experience in this common endeavour.

Many of these sources are documents, and documents written in African languages are coming to light. Thus, apart from Hausa, there are vast collections written in Fufulde, Kanuri, Nupe, and Dagbani. These are mainly 18th century documents, but they reflects a tradition of learning which goes back to the mediaeval times.

But our historical records do not consist alone in the facts which we committed in the Arabic script. Every society has methods of preserving facts about its past. And where a society has no literate traditions, it devises rigorous methods of oral recording. Scholars who have studied this phenomenon know this well. Historical recording in Africa therefore rightly comprises the documents in Arabic and African languages on the one hand, and, on the other, the well-preserved and authentic records of oral tradition. Our inheritance of oral literature, of epic and lyric poetry of stories and legends, praise songs and the chronicles of states Kings and dynasties preserved by palace officials, is of intrinsic interest and merit, as it is of historical importance.

The history of a nation is, unfortunately, too easily written as the history of its dominant class. If the history of a nation, of a people, cannot be found in the history of a class, how much less can the history of a continent be found in what is not even a part of it—Europe. And yet, this is precisely what many a European historian has done in the past. The history of Africa has with them been European centred. Africa was only the space in which Europe swelled up. The African past was ignored and dismissed in these tendentious works as not contributing to, or affecting the European expansion and presence in Africa.

If Africa's history is interpreted in terms of the interests of European merchandise and capital, missionaries and administrators, it is no wonder that African nationalism is regarded as a perversion and colonialism as a virtue.

You who are meeting here to-day in the First Congress of Africanists, are all representatives of various disciplines, and are determined to pool your immense knowledge of Africa for the progress of the African. Your efforts mark a renascence of scientific curiosity in the study of Africa and should be directed at an objective, impartial scrutiny and assessment of things African. While some of us are engaged with the political unification of Africa, Africanists everywhere must also help in building the spiritual and cultural foundations for the Unity of our Continent.

In East Africa, in the Sudan, in Egypt, in Nigeria, here in Ghana and elsewhere, the earth is being dug up apace–this time, not for gold or diamonds only, or for bauxite and other mineral riches, but also for its rich information about our past, its testimony to our achievements and its reformation of the sombre prophets of African History. Valuable pieces have already been unearthed, including evidence of the origin of man in Africa.

We have made our contribution to the fund of human knowledge by extending the frontiers or art, culture and spiritual values.

Democracy, for instance, has always been for us not a matter of technique, but more important than technique—a matter of socialist goals and aims. It was however, not only our socialist aims that were democratically inspired, but also the methods of their pursuit were socialist.

If we have lost touch with what our forefathers discovered and knew, this has been due to the system of education to which we were introduced. This system of education prepared us for a subservient role to Europe and things European. It was directed at estranging us from our own cultures in order the more effectively to serve a new and alien interest.

In rediscovering and revitalising our cultural and spiritual heritage and values, African Studies must help to redirect this new endeavour. The educational system which we devise to-day must equip us with the resources of a personality and a force strong enough to meet the intensities of the African presence and situation.

Education must enable us to understand correctly the strains and stresses to which Africa is subjected, to appreciate objectively the changes taking place, and enable us to contribute fully in a truly African spirit for the benefit of all, and for the peace and progress of the world.

African Studies is not a kind of academic hermitage. It has warm connections with similar studies in other countries of the world. It should change its course from anthropology to sociology, for it is the latter which more than any other aspect creates the firmest basis for social policy.

Your meeting here to-day as Africanists from various countries of the of the world, is truly historic. It emphasises the idea that knowledge transcends political and national boundaries. It is incumbent upon all Africanist scholars, all over the world , to work for a complete emancipation of the mind from all forms of domination, control and enslavement.

I cannot leave you to-day without referring to the distinction achieved by a Zulu student—Isaka Seme—when he won the first prize of the Curtis Medal Orations at Columbia University in the

5th of April, 1906. Distinguished Scholars, let me confess, with humility, that it is not my usual practice to quote others. On this occasion, however, I feel that I have a duty to place on record at this first Africanist Congress taking place here in Africa, the oration of Isaka Seme which, although made some fifty years ago, is still relevant to the postulates of our present situation in Africa.

With your indulgence, Distinguished Scholars, please bear with me while I quote his oration in full.

This is what he said:

"I have chosen to speak to you on this occasion upon 'The Regeneration of Africa'. I am an African, and I set my pride in my race over against a hostile public opinion. Men have tried to compare races on the basis of some equality. In all the works of nature, equality, if by it we mean identity, is an impossible dream! Search the universe! You will find no two units alike. The scientists tell us there are no two cells, no two atoms, identical. Nature has bestowed upon each a peculiar individuality, and exclusive patent—from the great giants of the forest to the tenderest blade. Catch in your hand, if you please, the gentle flakes of snow. Each is perfect gem, a new creation; it shines in its own glory—a work of art different from all of its aerial companions. Man, the crowning achievement of nature, defies analysis. He is a mystery through all ages and for all time. The races of mankind are composed of free and unique individuals. An attempt to compare them on the basis of equality can never be finally satisfactory. Each is self. My thesis stands on this truth; time has proved it. In all races genius is like a spark, which, concealed in the bosom of a flint, bursts forth at the summoning stroke. It may arise anywhere and in any race.

"I would ask you not to compare Africa to Europe or to any other continent. I make this request not from any fear that such comparison might bring humiliation upon Africa. The reason I have stated—a common standard is impossible! Come with me to the ancient capital of Egypt, Thebes, the city of one hundred gates. The grandeur of its venerable ruins and the gigantic proportions of its architecture reduce to insignificance the boasted monuments of other nations. The pyramids of Egypt are structures to which the world presents nothing comparable. The mighty monuments seem to look with disdain on every other work of human art and to vie with nature herself. All the glory of Egypt belongs to Africa and her people. These monuments are the indestructible memorials of their great and original genius. It is not through Egypt alone that Africa chains such unrivalled historic achievements. I could have spoken of the pyramids of Ethiopia, which, though inferior in size to those of Egypt, far surpass them in architectural beauty; their sepulchres which evince the highest purity taste, and of many prehistoric ruins in other arts of Africa. In such ruins in other parts of Africa. In such ruins Africa is like the golden sun, that, having sunk beneath the western horizon, still plays upon the world which he sustained and enlightened in his career.

"Justly, the world now demand:

"'Whither is fled the visionary gleam, Where is it now, the glory and the dream?

"Oh, for that historian who, with the open pen of truth, will bring to Africa's claim the strength of written proof. He will tell of a race whose onward tide was often swelled with tears, but in whose heart bondage has not quenched the fire of former years. He will write that in these later days when Earth's noble ones are named, she has a roll of honour too, of whom she is not ashamed. The giant is awakening!

"From the four corners of the earth Africa's sons, who have been proved through fire and sword, are marching to the future's golden door bearing the records of deeds of valour done.

"Mr. Calhoun, I believe, was the most philosophical of all the slave-holders. He said once that if he could find a black man who could understand the Greek syntax, he would then consider their race human, and his attitude toward enslaving them would therefore change. What might have been the sensation kindled by the Greek syntax in the mind of the famous Southerner, I have so far been unable to discover; but oh, I envy the moment that was lost! And woe to the tongues that refused to tell the truth! If any such were among the now living, I could show him among black men of pure African blood those who could repeat the Koran from memory, skilled in Latin, Greek and Hebrew–Arabic and Chaldaic—men great in wisdom and profound knowledge—one professor of philosophy in a celebrated German university; one corresponding member of the French Academy of sciences, who regularly transmitted to that society meteorological observations, and hydrographical journals and papers on botany and geology; another whom many ages call 'The Wise,' whose authority Mahomet himself frequently appealed to in the Koran in support of his own opinion–men of wealth and active benevolence, those whose distinguished talents and reputation have made them famous in the cabinet and in the field, officers of artillery in the great armies of Europe, generals and lieutenant-generals in the armies of Peter the Great in Russia and Napoleon in France, presidents of free republics, kings of independent nations which have burst their way to liberty by their own vigor. There are many other Africans who have shown marks of genius and high character sufficient to redeem their race from the charges which I am now considering.

"Ladies and Gentlemen, the day of great exploring expeditions in Africa is over! Man knows his home now in a sense never known before. Many great and holy men have evinced a passion for the day you are now witnessing—their prophetic vision shot through many unborn centuries to this very hour. 'Men shall run to and fro,' said Daniel, 'and knowledge shall increase upon the earth.' Oh, how true! see the triumph of human genius to-day! Science has searched out the deep things of nature, surprised the secrets of the most distant stars, disentombed the memorials of everlasting hills, taught the lightning to speak, the vapors to toil and the winds to worship—spanned the sweeping rivers, tunnelled the longest mountain range—made the world a vast whispering gallery, and has brought foreign nations into one civilized family. This all-powerful contact says even to the most backward race, you cannot remain where you are, you cannot fall back, you must advance! A great century has come upon us. N o race possessing the inherent capacity to survive can resist and remain unaffected by this influence of contact and intercourse, the backward with the advanced. This influence constitutes the very essence of efficient progress and of civilisation.

"From this heights of the twentieth century I again ask you to cast your eyes south of the Desert of Sahara. If you could go with me to the oppressed Congos and ask, What does it mean, that now, for liberty, they fight like men and die like martyrs; if you would go with me to Bechuanaland, face their council of headmen and ask what motives caused them recently to decree so emphatically that alcoholic drink shall not enter their country—visit their king, Khama, ask for what cause he leaves the gold and ivory palace of his ancestors, its mountain strongholds and all its august ceremony, to wander daily from any village to village through all his kingdom, without a guard or any decoration of his rank—a preacher of industry and education, and an apostle of the new order of things; if you would ask Menelik what means this that Abyssinia is now looking across the ocean—oh, if you could read the letters that come to us from Zululand—you too would be convinced that the elevation of the African race is evidently a part of the new order of things that belong to this new and powerful period.

"The African already recognizes his anomalous position and desires a change. The brighter day is rising upon Africa. Already I seem to see her chains dissolved, her desert plains red with harvest, her Abyssinia and her Zululand the seats of science and religion, reflecting the glory of the rising sun from the spires of their churches and universities. Her Congo and her Gambia whitened with commerce, her crowned cities sending forth the hum of business and all her sons employed in advancing the victories of peace—greater and more abiding than the spoils of war.

"Yes, the regeneration of Africa belongs to this new and powerful period! By this term regeneration I wish to be understood to mean the entrance into a new life, embracing the diverse phases of a higher, complex existence. The basic factor which assures their regeneration resides in the awakened race-consciousness. This gives them a clear perception of their elemental needs and of their undeveloped powers. It therefore must lead them to the attainment of that higher and advanced standard of life.

"The African people, although not a strictly homogeneous race, possess a common fundamental sentiment which is everywhere manifest, crystallizing itself into one common controlling idea.

Conflicts and strife are rapidly disappearing before the fusing force of this enlightened perception of the true intertribal relation, which relation should subsist among a people with a common destiny. Agencies of a social economic and religious advance tell of a new spirit which, acting as a leavening ferment, shall raise the anxious and aspiring mass to the level of their ancient glory. The ancestral greatness, the unimpaired genius, and the recuperative power of the race, its irrepressibility, which assures its permanence, constitute the African's greatest source of inspiration. He has refused to camp forever on the borders of the industrial world; having learned that knowledge is power, he is educating his children. You find them in Edinburgh, in Cambridge, and in the great schools of Germany. These return to their country like arrow, to drive darkness from the land. I hold that his industrial an educational initiative, and his untiring devotion to these activities, must be regarded as positive evidences of this process of is regeneration.

"The regeneration of Africa means that a new and unique civilization is soon to be added to the world. The African is not a proletarian in the world of science and art. He has precious creations of his own, of ivory, of copper and of gold, fine, plate willow-ware and weapons of superior workmanship. Civilization resembles an organic being in its development—it is born, it perishes, and it can propagate itself. More particularly, it resembles a plant, it takes root in the teeming earth, and when the seeds fall in other soils new varieties sprout up. The most essential departure of this new civilization is that it shall be thoroughly spiritual and humanistic—indeed a regeneration moral and eternal!

> O Africa !
> Like some great century plant that shall bloom
> In ages hence, we watch thee; in our dream
> See in thy swamps the Prospero of our stream;
> Thy doors unlocked, where knowledge in her tomb
> Hath lain innumerable years in gloom.
> Then shalt thou, walking with that morning gleam,
> Shine as thy sister lands with equal beam."

Distinguished Scholars: on behalf of myself and the Government and people of Ghana, it is my great pleasure to welcome you to Ghana and to this first Africanists Conference to be held in Africa. I wish you every success.

22
SOME NOTABLE QUOTATIONS

- "We Africans mean to be masters on our own continent"

- "Let us tell the Colonialists and neo-Colonialists, that moderate or radical, militant or reasonable, Africa is Africa, one and indivisible. It is not their business to categorise our attributes. That is for our African masses to do, and they will do it in a manner that will spell unity and not division."

- "...We who are here today pay tribute to the memories of those of those who have fallen in this noble cause of national freedom. We must give every possible encouragement we can to African Freedom Fighters to whom we are linked by a common destiny...

- "...The imperialists of today endeavour to achieve their ends not merely by military means, but by economic penetration, cultural assimilation, ideological domination, psychological infiltration, and subversive activities...

- "...To-day we are one. If in the past the Sahara divided us, now it unites us. And an injury to one is an injury to all of us. From this Conference must go out a new message: 'Hands off Africa! Africa must be Free !' "

- "So long as Colonialism exists in Africa, Africans cannot help taking the way we do now, and mankind cannot escape the constant threat of war."

- "History has described to us the tragedies which have beset every other continent upon this planet—the international wars, the rebellions and revolutions. We must be determined that this continent of ours shall not repeat that dismal history. The continent of Africa has been drenched in blood in the past; it has been raided for slaves; it has been partitioned and exploited and looted. Precisely because it has had this kind of past it is determined not to have that kind of future. If we succeed, and succeed we must, the whole of mankind—not Africa alone—will reap immense benefits."

- "Africa marches on relentlessly to its cherished goal of independence and unity and none can stem the tide any longer. It is therefore up to all of us to contribute our share to facilitate this momentum so that generations after us will be blessed."

- "Always the most oppressed, the slavery and misery of colonial oppression stung our African women into action, and they still remain in the front line of the battle in ever-increasing numbers."

www.ingramcontent.com/pod-product-compliance
Lightning Source LLC
Chambersburg PA
CBHW061449300426
44114CB00014B/1907